HOOK UP

A COMPLETE GUIDE TO SOUTHERN CALIFORNIA OCEAN SPORTFISHING

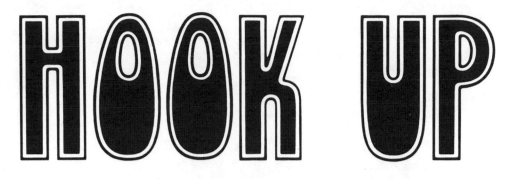

HOOK UP

A Complete Guide
to Southern California
Ocean Sportfishing

by
CHARLIE DAVIS

Illustrations by Steven Davis

To my family. My wife, Helen; my daughter Diann, and my sons Steven and Mark, for patience, understanding and assistance.

Library of Congress Catalog Number: 77-71288
ISBN: 0-916682-05-6

**Library of Congress Cataloging in Publication
Data**

Davis, J   Charles
  Hook up.

  Includes index.
  1. Saltwater fishing — California, Southern.
  2. Fishing — California, Southern.   I.   Title.
  SH473.D38   799.1's   77-71288
  ISBN 0-916682-05-6

For information address:
Charles Davis
16302 Wildfire Circle
Huntington Beach, California 92649

Printed in the United States of America

Cover photo by Bill Beebe

Back cover photo by Gene Henry

PRINTING HISTORY
1st Printing March 1977
2nd Printing May 1977
3rd Printing November 1977
4th Printing September 1978
5th Printing September 1979
6th Printing October 1980
7th Printing January 1981

Forword

When Charlie Davis asked me to write the foreward to this book, I was immensely flattered, as I believe him to be one of the finest, most dedicated, and hardest working anglers in the world.

Although a number of books on Southern California ocean sport fishing have been written, they have neither the abundance of accurate information nor the credentials of this one.

As time progresses, marine angling becomes more and more difficult at a rate faster than even modern technology can match. Despite synthetic lines, fiberglass and graphite rods, fathometers, long range boats, downriggers, and all the other aids in the catching of fish, it is still know-how that does the job. How to read water and weather, seeing fish and birds working, matching the lure or the bait to the water and the quarry, tying knots, chumming correctly, trolling methods, and a myriad of other skills necessary to success have heretofore never been available to this degree in print. This is fisherman talk directed at fishermen who might otherwise have had to learn many of these things the hard way over a period of years at the cost of many a lost or unhooked fish.

Another important facet to this book is fish identification and nomenclature. As many of you anglers know, non-generic fish names seem to change every thirty miles up the coast, especially the rock fishes. There are many excellent photographs of freshly caught fish to aid in this identification and the various common usage names to match them, a distinct improvement over line drawings and black and white photos of dried-out specimens.

The name of the game is *lore*, and there is more fishing lore in this volume than any I have ever had the pleasure of reading.

We should all thank Charlie Davis for the public service that his many years of work has produced. No matter how long and hard a person has fished in the sea, he will learn something from this treatise.

Timothy M. Doheny
Past President
Fish and Game Commission
State of California

Acknowledgments

It took the better part of two and a half years to put this book together. During that time I received a great deal of help and encouragement, without which it is doubtful that "HOOK UP" would have become a reality. I wish to take this opportunity to express my heartfelt appreciation to those who helped.

Captain Bruce Barnes of the Qualifier 105, Captain "Big John" Worobieff of the Ranger 85, Captain Garry Black of the Conquest, Captain Eddie McEwen of the Pacitic Queen and Captain Frank LoPreste of the Searcher for patient assistance in obtaining on-the-water photographs and for the fine fishing that produced those photos.

Bill Beebe, Al Tetzlaff, Nick Curcione, Neff Nash, Paul Albrecht, Ron Howarth and Dr. Bob McCoy for providing outstanding photographs from their collections.

Ilda Bonar for her expert preparation of the manuscript.

Fay Ainsworth and Pam Kowalski of Outdoor Empire Publishing Company for their patience and expertise in putting the manuscript and photographs together. Jack Main for technical assistance.

Bill Nott, of Sportfishing Association of California for statistical information.

And finally, to Bill Farden for having faith in the project from the beginning.

Charlie Davis
Carson, California
December 1, 1976

About This Book

There are many fine books that detail fishing methods, tackle and fish. I have read many and found them most helpful. However, I have been unable to find a book devoted to my own fishing grounds – the Southern California and western Baja coast. This area, from Point Conception on the north to Cabo San Lucas on the south, is the subject of this book. It is intended to pass along knowledge and tips I have learned in fishing this area for over 40 years. During this period fish and fishing have changed tremendously and I will attempt to show you the way it used to be as well as how it is today.

To write this book it was necessary for me to answer the question: "What is sportfishing?" My reply is that sportfishing is any fishing that provides recreation to an individual angler. It is not necessary to do battle with leviathans on the offshore grounds; neither is it limited to the tournament angler. All who fish for sport are brothers although their methods and prey may differ. It has been my good fortune to enjoy this sport in California since I was a small boy, and I have come to believe that the name of the game is whatever you like to do: surf, pier, barge, small boat inshore fishing, or trolling for marlin and baiting broadbill offshore. All aspects of fishing and fish available to the Southern California angler are what I will talk about.

For the casual reader who merely wishes to be entertained, this book will undoubtedly be a bore, for I have tried to detail all the tricks I have learned over a span of 40 years. This book is for today's angler; one who had no opportunity to tap the fish-filled waters of yesterday and, thereby, develop these skills. All tips in this book have been acquired by personal experience unless otherwise stated. The information has been gained from first-hand experience as a sportfisherman, deckhand and skipper, commercial fisherman and teacher.

I hope this book may answer some of the questions and solve some of the problems of the sportfisherman.

Table of Contents

The author's daughter, Diann, with a "fast-taper" rod.

". . .for a couple of years, so help me, our most popular line color was pink?"

Chapter 1
The Tackle

The tackle used for saltwater fishing in Southern California and Baja waters varies greatly with the type of fish sought, size of bait used and feeding moods of the fish. One outfit can suffice for pier, surf and most live bait fishing. This can be either a conventional or spinning outfit with about 20-pound line and a medium action rod of 7½ to 8 feet. The Penn "Beachmaster" reel, number 155 or 160 is a good choice, or the take-a-part 150 and 200 "Surfmasters." For longer casts, I prefer the Newell 229F because of the ball bearing feature, and higher gear ratio.

While there are a number of fine salt water spinning reels on the market, I recommend them only for surf, pier and inshore fishing. They simply do not work with large fish that make long runs. While such fish have been taken on spinning reels, more of them are lost than are landed. Spinning reels are best for surfcasting, pier fishing and casting light baits and lures for small- to moderate-sized fish such as barracuda, bass, bonito and halibut.

For the serious fisherman, several categories of tackle are important. It might be advantageous to discuss the tackle I usually take on a sportfishing trip out of San Diego or other Southern California ports.

I usually have a light outfit with a 6-foot, fast-taper rod and a small reel, like the 220F Newell loaded with 12-pound test mono. Then a second outfit with 20-pound mono and a larger reel—say the 229F Newell. This is in combination with a 7-foot, light tip, fast-taper rod. These are my two basic live bait rigs.

I will also have a Newell 340F reel full of 40-pound mono on a rod of about 8 feet for a slower, more parabolic action. This is the "jig stick" for throwing aluminum "candy bar" type jigs. This rod also serves

as a bait outfit when the fishing really gets good. If I expect to be using squid for bait, I will have another outfit with a Newell 229F full of 30-pound mono. This is a good outfit for albacore. Finally, I will have a sturdy rod of about 6½ feet with a roller top and either a 4/0 or 6/0 Penn or Newell reel. I prefer the high speed model, since I like to fish rock cod in the off season, and the 6/0 makes a good cod reel with the addition of the extension handle.

For live bait boat fishing I have a 447F Newell full of 50-pound test mono. This outfit is used for trolling albacore, tuna or marlin and is handy if a black sea bass shows up or for that infrequent occasion when albacore attack the boat in a wide open bite. I also use this general purpose rig for "yo-yo" jig fishing with heavy jigs to 14 ounces.

These five outfits will handle almost any condition you are likely to encounter. For long range trips into Mexican waters the same basic outfits apply, but I have a couple of 4/0 hi-speed Newell reels loaded with 50-pound mono for heavy duty jigging and bait fishing larger tuna.

I own and use both Penn and Newell reels, and I have coverted all of my Penn reels with Newell parts, wherever available. The use of Newell's spools, posts and reelstands both lightens and strengthens the reels, and in many cases increases line capacity. Penn is now furnishing aluminum spools for many of their reels, too. I prefer aluminum spools over either plastic of brass, chrome plated models, as I believe that they are far stronger, as well as much lighter in weight, therefore providing a much better casting reel. By converting to an aluminum spool, for example, I find that I can convert what was a heavy trolling model reel

Penn No. 500 Jigmaster

Penn No. 140 Squidder

Penn No. 113 Senator 4/0

into one which can be used for casting jigs and heavy baits, as well as trolling. Newell currently manufactures spools for most Penn reels up to and including the 6/0 size, as well as manufacturing his own reels with up to 6/0 line capacity. His larger reels have proven themselves on marlin and broadbill during the past several years.

There are a number of rod makers who produce rods specifically designed for West Coast fishing. Rods range in price from very inexpensive to well over $100. Generally speaking, the angler gets what he pays for. There are well-designed and beautifully-made production rods available through tackle stores. The specialty tackle shop can make custom rods to order with fancy wraps, heavy applications of finish (for a very high gloss) with colors and diamond wraps to suit the most discriminating angler.

The beginning angler should rent tackle at the landing or pier of his choice, go fishing and observe other anglers and their equipment. Make a couple of trips before investing in tackle that may not be exactly what's desired. Pick a good tackle outlet where the help has some knowledge of local conditions; they can be most helpful to a beginner.

For most fishing I prefer rods that have a fairly fast taper rather than the parabolic models that have a continuous bend clear down to the reelseat. I do not like the extreme tapers with the very fine tip that have a "floppy" feel when whipped back and forth. Most of this is personal preference which develops as one does more and more fishing. I do not believe that the perfect fishing rod has yet been made and though I have helped design rods, I am always looking for something better. Parabolic rods are easier on the fisherman but they are also easier on the fish. I have found fast-taper rods, within reason, whip a fish much faster even though they make the angler work a little harder. I like a parabolic action rod for throwing heavy jigs or sinkers long distances. They are comfortable to cast, and the timing is much slower, resulting in an easier cast with fewer backlashes.

The better rods have good hardware – double locking, chromed reelseats; bridged guides; carboloy or ceramic tip tops; and wrappings well coated with a durable finish of expoxy or equal material. Fittings have recently been developed with ceramic and aluminum oxide rings. These show great promise, since they are diamond hard and extremely smooth.

Many rods are now being manufactured out of the new space age material – graphite.

Graphite material, as it is used, consists of pure carbon graphite fibers, woven into a cloth and then impregnated with a plastic matrix, epoxy resin. This cloth is then cut into a pattern and rolled onto a mandrel in much the same manner as in the manufacture of fiberglass rods. The composition of the graphite fibers is such, however, that entirely different patterns and mandrels must be used, along with some variation in manufacturing techniques.

Graphite has a much higher modulus, or resistance to bending. This means that rods made of "high modulus graphite" are much lighter than comparable rods of fiberglass. (As much as forty percent.) Graphite is much stronger than fiberglass, approaching the strength of high quality steel, so much less material can be used in the graphite rod. High modulus means that the rods come back to the normal, straight configuration, from a bent configuration, faster than any other material found. For the fisherman, this means farther, faster and more accurate casts, plus a much more delicate "feel" of what is happening on the end of the line.

Because of the continuing high cost of graphite cloth, it has been found that a blend, or "composite" of graphite and fiberglass fibers can produce rods with most of the qualities of graphite, but with significant reductions in costs. The resulting rods are much lighter in weight than comparable rods of fiberglass, and yet retain most of the sensitivity of graphite. Another fairly new development is the use of a fiberglass cloth called "s" glass in rod manufacture. This material is used to produce rods that are lighter in weight than standard fiberglass, and with much of the sensitivity of graphite. There are now reelseats being manufactured of combinations of graphite and stainless steel that are much lighter than brass, chrome plated models that are familiar on most rods, that seem to hold up equally well, again, reducing rod weight. These new developments in lightweight reels, rods and components give today's anglers greatly improved tackle over that which was available at the time of the first printing of this book just a few short years ago.

At this writing, rods of graphite construction are considerably more expensive than rods of fiber-

Newell aluminum spool conversion parts.

glass, but offer many advantages. Most of the major rod manufacturers, worldwide, have some graphite rods in production, or have announced graphite rods for the future. Graphite is here to stay, and will have a definite impact on fishing in the future.

As for line, most anglers use monofilament exclusively for live bait boat fishing. The exceptions are for bottom fishing in deep water, as will be discussed in the rock cod chapter and a few club tournaments that still specify dacron or linen line, but this is merely a carryover from the old days. Monofilament line is superior in almost all respects—except for stretch. This stretch, too, can be a plus in the angler's favor by acting as a shock absorber on big fish. I still like dacron for trolling because the lack of stretch helps to set the hook, but for all other surface fishing I use monofilament.

There are, of course, many fine brands of monofilament on the market. The recent trend has been toward clear mono because, I suppose, clear line tends to assume the color of the water and, therefore be less visible. However, I cannot truthfully say that I have found much difference in the effect of color. During the past twenty years I have seen and fished with almost every conceivable color of line. For a while, a blue line the color of channel water was the color; then it was clear; only to be replaced by smoke gray or dull green for a few years. For a couple of years, so help me, it was pink! I used this pink line and it was fine—no better, mind you, than other colors, but it worked just as well. The theory introduced was that fish cannot see pink!

I have found that softness, suppleness—whatever term you wish to use—coupled with good knot strength, are much more important factors than color. It seems that when the line is too soft it loses something in knot strength. Personally, I like the idea of fluorescent line. It is easy for the angler or

A standard Penn 4/0 reel [lower] with Newell conversion, a "broadbill special" [upper].

deckhand to see and yet seems to be just as invisible in the water as any other line. This is a definite advantage as you can see the line move as soon as a fish picks up the bait.

As I mentioned, you get what you pay for. Cheap line is never a bargain. Line is not really expensive and, when compared to the investment in the rest of the gear and cost of a fishing trip, the best line appears very reasonable. I try never to fish with the same line more than one season but I fish an average of one day each week, year-round. Sunlight is the worst enemy of monofilament, so be careful to store your reels where the sun cannot reach them. It is not necessary to wash or dry monofilament line, because it does not rot or mildew as the linen lines of yesterday, but I always rinse my reels in fresh water at the end of a trip, being careful not to get water inside the reels. Monofilament line absorbs water. For this reason, line that has been soaked overnight, or used the day before, will come off the reel much more smoothly than dry line.

Converting Penn Reels

There have been some significant improvements in reel parts that enable the angler to improve reels for West Coast use.

Carl Newell of Glendale, California, has perfected aluminum spools that are about the same weight as the plastic spools furnished with most models, and are strongert than the brass spools furnished with the heavy duty style reels.

By replacing the factory spools with Newell spools, the angler achieves the capability of (1) casting the same as with the plastic spools, as necessary for flyline fishing with live bait, and (2) with the strength to resist the pressure that stretched monofilament puts on a spool when fighting heavy fish. Newell has also made a number of innovative spools that enable the angler to take advantage of the great Penn Reel drag system while using a lightweight outfit. This is great for fighting heavy fish such as yellowfin tuna and billfish, often caught on the long-range trips.

There are also spools available for the size 3/0 Senator model reel that increase the line capacity by 18 percent. It is necessary to install the longer Penn #500 posts and reel stand to achieve the widths for this spool. There are two spools available for the 4/0 Senator. The first makes what Newell describes as the "Marlin Special" and also increases the line capacity by 18 percent. The other is the "Broadbill Special" which increases the capacity by 39 percent. The 500 Jigmaster can be enlarged to accept 15 percent more line. Newell also manufactures a kit for the 6/0, called the "Black Marlin Special", which lightens the reel as well as increasing line capacity to approximately that of a 9/0 size reel. A number of broadbill swordfish have been landed with this conversion in recent years. In each case because of the additional width, it is necessary to install the longer posts and reelstand from Newell. Most long-range fishermen, along with many local anglers, have found these reels to be the answer for larger fish. I have used them since their inception and I wouldn't leave shore without them. In fact, I have converted all of my reels for both heavy and light fishing. *Since the first printing of this book, Carl Newell has moved into the manufacturing of complete reels. These reels are designed for live bait fishing and long range trips, and feature light weight, fast retrieves up to 5 to 1 and extreme balance for long casts.* There are now Newell reels to fit almost any fishing situation to be encountered in Southern California and Baja, from very light line models up to 80-pound test. All have the option of 5 to 1 retrieve, which I prefer.

The Daiwa Corporation has also moved into the area of saltwater reel manufacture, since the first publication of this book, and now manufactures a complete line of reels, up to size 9/0. These reels feature aluminum spools and fast retrieve.

For additional information on Newell parts and conversion kits, write to: Carl Newell Mfg. Co., 940 Allen St., Glendale, Ca. 91209.

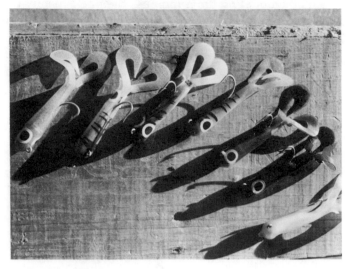

Sevenstrand's new Clout Lures have proven to be very effective, with or without squid.

Egg-shaped sliding sinkers [upper left]. Clinch on sinkers [center]. Rubbercore [lower right].

In recent years the use of squid for bait has increased in popularity. This is the author's favorite method of hooking this bait.

"Live bait fishing. . .is one of the most productive methods in the world."

Chapter 2
The Methods

Live bait fishing as it is practiced along the California coast is one of the most productive methods of fishing in the world. The beginning in Southern California in the early 1920's was due to the plentiful supply of sardines and anchovies. Some enterprising boat owners installed large tanks, equipped with pumps to supply circulating water, on the sterns of their boats, where bait could be kept alive for weeks. It was quickly learned that a light but steady supply of this bait thrown over the side would induce the fish to a feeding mood and hold them close to the boat. Chumming soon became an art. As a result, anglers using live bait met with great success.

Over the years, tackle has been manufactured specifically for this type of fishing. Because the baits are light and difficult to cast with heavy metal spools, Penn reels were made with bakelite plastic spools. Soon special reels were designed for casting the light baits and innovative rods followed. Early fishermen used "Calcutta" cane rods as long as 11 feet to cast bait well away from the boat. More affluent fishermen used split bamboo. In the late 1940's, rods of fiberglass were introduced and these rods have become so popular that other types are now seldom seen.

For live bait fishing, most anglers use reels with either the lightweight plastic or the new aluminum spools, and monofilament line of from 10-pound test to 50-pound test, depending on the size of both the bait used and the fish sought. Rods range from six feet to nine feet in length. The best live bait rods have a very light tip, sometimes as small as a size six tip top, and taper rather rapidly to a large butt diameter. They are usually called "fast taper" rods. A light tip gives

the necessary action to cast the bait while the heavier, lower section allows the angler to beat the fish in a reasonable length of time. The older style "parabolic" action rods cast a bait well, and will cause less backlashes when casting jigs. In addition, short, parabolic rods have proven to be the very best for fighting very large fish from a standing position, and from a dead boat.

In live bait fishing it is important to have the bait look as natural as possible. Frequently, the water is exceptionally clear and fish can be very "choosy." Selection of a bait from the bait tank many times makes the difference between a bulging sack of fish or an empty one. When choosing an anchovy, it is wise to take the time to pick the strongest and liveliest. Remember that your bait must carry the hook and drag your line. The best anchovy is one that has all its scales, does not have a red nose or sides and wears a metallic green cast on its back. The dull blue baits are usually sluggish, and are poor selections.

In fishing from an anchored or drifting boat, the bait is usually "collar hooked." A good tip: learn to pick your bait with your left hand, if you are righthanded, so that when you get to your rod you will not have to change hands to hook the bait. Slip your hand into the bait well and let the bait you have chosen swim across your hand; then lift your hand easily and the bait will usually end up in your palm. The anchovy should be on its side with the tail down and the head between the thumb and forefinger. Don't squeeze the bait—just hold it loosely cupped in your hand. Hook it lightly behind the gill cover and get it into the water as soon as possible. If you should drop your bait on your way from the bait tank, discard it and start over. By the time you recover the bait off the deck it will probably be tired and listless.

Another method of hooking the bait is through the nose. Bring the point of the hook up through the tip of the jaw and out the top of the nose and well ahead of the eyes. For fish on the surface that are "boiling" on the chum, "flylining" is the best method of presenting the bait. This means fishing without any weight or sinker on the line—just the hook and the bait. Since the anchovy weighs but a fraction of an ounce, casting becomes an art and takes a lot of practice. A spring-type clothespin weighs about the same as a medium sized anchovy and makes a good substitute, when practicing.

Once the bait is cast, the reel is left in free spool and the bait is allowed to run. If the bait runs toward you, the line may be retrieved by spinning the spool with the thumbs. When a fish picks up the bait, a short run is allowed before setting the hook. With some fish, particularly calico bass and barracuda, it is often necessary to let the fish run, then stop and turn the bait before setting the hook on the second run. With the larger pelagic fish, such as tuna and albacore, it is not good to let the fish run with the bait since they may spit it out. The rule here is that when you think you have a bite, set the hook. These fish "inhale" the bait when they take it.

Many times I have stood next to a fisherman, watched and listened as a fish took the bait, then heard the fisherman say, "I've got a strike," and watched as the hook was set—too late! When in doubt, put the reel in gear and swing!

A word of caution: Always be sure the drag setting on your reel is appropriate to the line being used. Many of the fish common to these waters will take well over 100 yards of line on the first run and, if the drag is so tight they cannot run, a broken line will result. It is a rare occurence for any of our fish to "spool" an angler but too many fishermen seem reluctant about using the line on their reel. Normally the reel will have from 200 to 300 yards of line and a great many fish are lost each season because the angler simply puts too much pressure on at the beginning of the fight.

Another thing to remember is that the spool diameter decreases as the fish runs and, as a result, the drag pressure increases. On a fish making a long run it is best to decrease the drag pressure rather than to increase it. When the fish has stopped and settled down, then the drag may be adjusted.

Often, Spanish mackerel, green mackerel and sardines are used for bait. All work well for yellowtail, large calico bass, white sea bass and some other fish. Large bait requires large hooks, 2/0 to 6/0, heavier lines than for anchovies, and a heavier rod to cast and set the hook. In order to hook a fish it is necessary to tear the hook through the bait and, in the case of mackerel and sardines, this takes some doing! No light hand here—point the rod at the fish while it is running, then throw the reel in gear and swing hard several times. If you doubt whether the bait is running hard, or has been picked up by a fish, a light thumb pressure on the spool will usually indicate the difference. If it is just the bait running you will feel the quiver of the swimming; if it is a fish, it will be smooth running, so—swing!

In recent years, the use of squid for bait has increased in popularity because, at certain times, it is the main diet of most fish in our waters. Squid are sometimes difficult to find, but are well worth the effort. Early in the year, when fishing white sea bass and yellowtail, boats lucky enough to have live squid in their bait tanks are often the only ones

In fishing from an anchored or drifting boat, anchovies are usually "collar hooked".

returning to the docks with fish.

Almost all fish common to the California coast relish squid. Large calico bass and all bottom fish, as well as the larger game fish, show a definite preference for this bait. Squid are caught at night when they are attracted to bright lights hung over the sides of boats. When they are thick, during spawning season, they are simply scooped into the bait tanks with large dip nets or brails. At times, it is necessary to catch them by hook and line in order to have enough bait to fish the day. Recently, it was discovered that certain glow in the dark plastic "Squid jigs" have proven very effective for this purpose.

These lures are manufactured in the Orient, and are really phenomenal. They outperform chrome sinkers and "Lucky Joe" or "Handy Dandy" types 20 or 30 to one. They have a number of needle-sharp, barbless hooks that make it almost impossible for the squid to escape, but also make it easy to unhook the squid by simply tipping the lure upside down. When squid spawn, they place the spawn sacks in clusters, held together with a sticky "glue." The "Squid Catcher" lure looks like an unattached egg sack and squid try to take it to a cluster. It really works, and every serious angler should keep a few in his tackle box.

Squid will also strike at chromed sinkers and may be caught by attaching a treble hook and jigging the sinker up and down. Snag lines of brightly colored feathers are sometimes effective.

When using squid for bait it is normal to use some type of sinker ahead of the hook. I prefer the egg-shaped sliding sinker, placed free on the line ahead of the hook. This have proven most effective for me and for my family when chasing yellowtail and white sea bass. Sinker size varies, according to water depth and current conditions.

Several years ago it was discovered that instead of a sinker, a leadhead green jig worked extremely well, with the squid, for calico bass and other fish. The green color seems to approximate the color of the spawn and triggers a feeding instinct. Curly tailed Leadhead such as Clouts and Scampis work very well with squid, alive, whole or in pieces.

When fish are feeding on squid, large hooks, 4/0 and 5/0, are the rule. Squid is a very soft bait and is easily cast off the hook, and a large hook has proven to be helpful in preventing this. The best method is to cast the squid out, let it settle on the bottom, and then retrieve it in erratic stop-and-go motions. Fish will usually strike as the bait is sinking. If they do not, it takes the erratic retreive to get a strike. A short run is the rule before setting the hook.

I have told my fishing classes there is no way for a person to like putting a live squid on the hook for the first time. Squid are equipped with 10 legs and a small parrot-like beak. While you are trying to put the hook in the squid, it will be doing its best to wrap all 10 legs around your hand and nip you with its beak. A big, active squid can nip hard enough to make you jump but will rarely draw blood. Still, if you are at all squeamish, putting a squid on the hook can be a traumatic experience. Once you find out what a good bait squid is, the trauma usually disappears. Always hook squid through the pointed tail. To avoid the trauma of having a live squid wrap it's tentacles around your hand, squirt ink on you and nip you with it's beak, bait your hook as follows: Hold the animal with its head in the center of the palm of your left hand (if you are right handed), and close your hand over it's head. That way, the tail will be exposed for the placement of the hook, and the "business end" will be incapacitated. Once you have the squid on your hook, be careful where you point it, however, since it can "shoot" it's load of water and ink at any time,

One method of nose hooking in anchovy.

Typical "nose hook" with anchovy.

while you are preparing to cast, and your neighbor or fishing partner will not appreciate it if he catches the load.

Because they die shortly after spawning, and are usually caught during spawning runs, squid do not live well either in receivers or in bait tanks. During periods of full moon or at other times when they're difficult to find, fresh dead or frozen squid are very effective bait. Use them like live bait, or cut them into pieces. The head is usually the best part.

There are other baits occasionally found in bait tanks, with anchovies, that are good for some varieties of fish. These include small perch, queenfish (herring) and white croaker (tom cod), which are all good bass baits. Smelt and grunion are sometimes attractive to yellowtail, barracuda and bass. Smelt are usually hooked through the nose, while herring, perch and tom cod are best hooked across the pelvic fins.

Knots

Entire books have been written on the subject of knots. We, however, will concern ourselves with only the basic knots which we have found necessary for fishing purposes—how the knot is tied, its use, and the comparative breaking strengths.

Starting with the Palomar knot, it is one of the newer knots and is the one that should be used for most ties of hooks or swivels to the end of the line. The Palomar, property tied, is one of the few knots which will not slip and which gives 100 percent strength. This is an easy knot to master and I use it routinely for most of my ties, with the exception of heavy monofilament where it does not work well.

The dropper loop or Blood knot is a very easy knot to master and has many uses. It is used to tie two lines of equal (or nearly equal) size together to make tapered leaders and make a dropper loop. I also use it to make rock cod gangions by inserting the ring of a swivel into the crossed lines instead of the loop. The skippers and deckhands use the Blood knot to save many a fish in hot fishing conditions when a fish gets under the boat. They pick up the line on the opposite side from the angler, cut the line and hold it until the fisherman can get around for a quick tie to rejoin him to his fish. This tie can be made in seconds. The Blood knot reduces line strength by 15 percent.

For fishing with bait I prefer to "Snell" my hooks onto monofilament. The Snell knot is not easy to learn, but once mastered, it is fast and fooolproof and, most importantly, the Snell will help you hook fish. To tie the Snell properly the line must be put through the eye of the hook from the side on which the point is located. This forces the point of the hook into the fish when tension is applied. Once through the eye, form a loop, and, with the hook held between thumb and forefinger with the point of the hook toward thumbnail, lay the lines along the shank of the hook with the loop down.

The bitter end of the line should extend past the bend of the hook for an inch or so. Next, pass the loop six or seven times around the shank of the hook and the two parts of line that are lying along the shank. I do this by putting my first two fingers into the loop. After making the turns and while still holding the lines against the shank, draw the running end of the line tight and then draw the tag, or bitter end, tight with your teeth. The advantages of the Snell are multifold: it won't slip, is usually as strong as the Palomar, and because of the rocking motion imparted to the hook, setting is improved over a straight tie.

The next knot is the one generally used on the West Coast. I am speaking of the Improved Clinch knot. When properly tied this knot will hold well. If the line is passed around six or more times, the improved clinch knot will test at 100 percent and will not slip. A good insurance against slipping is to wet the line first and pull it firmly to test.

For double lines, I use one of two knots, the "Bimini Hitch", and the "Quadruple Overhand". The Bimini Hitch is also called the "Twenty Times Around Knot", and is a bit complicated to tie. After the line has been doubled to the desired length, the end loop is twisted twenty times. Next, the loop is spread, while holding the bitter end fast to the running line. Once the loop has been spread to where the bitter end lays along the running line, the bitter end is wrapped back over the resulting twists, and then half hitched numerous times to both legs of the doubled line, and finished with half hitches over both legs of the doubled line. This knot is best tied by two people, although, with practice, it can be done by one. I have tested the Bimini many times and have found it to be a 100% knot. For monofilament, I generally use the quadruple overhand, which is simply an overhand knot, with the loop passed through four times. This knot gives great strength, close to 100%, and is easily tied.

So there you have it—knots that will get you out of almost any fishing problem. The Palomar to tie hooks or swivels on the line or leader; Blood knot to join two lines or make dropper loops; Snell for bait fishing; Improved Clinch knot for general use; Bimini Hitch for making a loop. This just about covers it.

How To Rig Wire

Although wire is not as important in Southern California today as it used to be, it is still most important in Mexico and all tropical waters. Two basic types of wire are used—singlestrand stainless piano wire and stranded wire consisting of either 7 strands or 49 strands.

PALOMAR KNOT

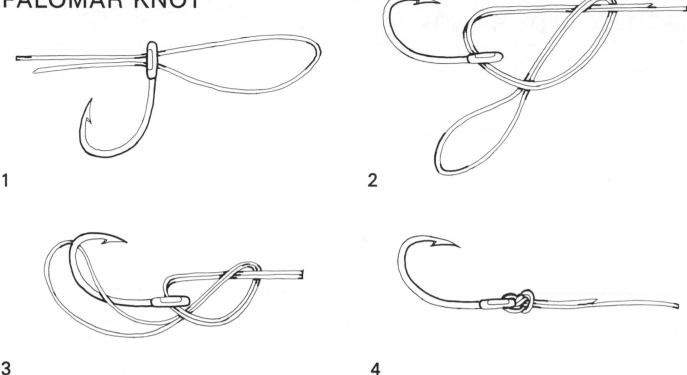

1

2

3

4

The palomar, properly tied is one of the few knots which will not slip and gives 100% strength.

Single strand wire is handy for making short bait or lure leaders because it is easy to tie and does not kink easily in short lengths. To tie, bring the wire through the eye of the hook or swivel and bend into a loop. Then, the two resulting wires are twisted around each other to form a series of "X's." After six or seven twists, the remaining wire is wrapped tightly back over the x's for six or seven turns. Then, most importantly, the remaining tag end is bent at a right angle to the main wire to make a little crank handle – wind up this crank and the wire will break cleanly at the main wire. This will not leave a cutting projection as will a wire clipped off with cutting pliers and the "x's" will prevent the wire from slipping down on the ring. Try it.

Stranded wire should be secured with brass sleeves. Seven strand and 49 strand wire is too flexible to tie by wrapping except by machine. The annealed brass sleeves furnished by Sevenstrand do an excellent job of securing this wire.

The wire is secured in the following manner: after making certain that the sleeves will accept two pieces of wire, two sleeves are slid onto the wire and a loop is formed with a simple overhand knot. Then, pass the tag end of the wire through the loop a second time and slide the crimping sleeves down over the tag end and crimp. Crimp each of the sleeves twice and cut the excess wire as close as possible.

When using swimming – plug type lures, the leaders should be shortened and retied after each few hours of trolling. Wire tends to fracture, and monofilament will wear.

On very large mono (250-pound test and up) crimping sleeves are also recommended. The larger mono does not tie well.

Fighting Techniques

I believe the difference between a great angler and one who is somewhat less than great can be measured by the manner in which he fights a fish. There is a very fine line which, once passed over, results in broken gear. The accomplished angler fights the fish right on the edge of this line – applying all the pressure that his tackle will allow, short of breakage. This takes practice – learning just what the tackle will stand, and it also takes angling technique. Each fisherman has to learn for himself the limits of his tackle. The only way to learn is to fish, and fish hard – hard enough to break off some fish and find out exactly where this fine line lies. This can't be taught, it has to be experienced.

There are some tips I can pass along, however, that will make it easier to fight the larger gamefish.

Test your tackle before you go fishing; find out just how much it will take. Thread your rod and tie the line to the bumper of your car or a fence post, and

IMPROVED CLINCH KNOT

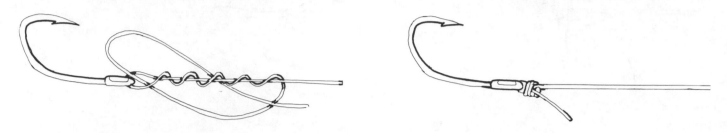

If the line is passed around six or more times this knot will test at 100% and will not slip.

BLOOD KNOT

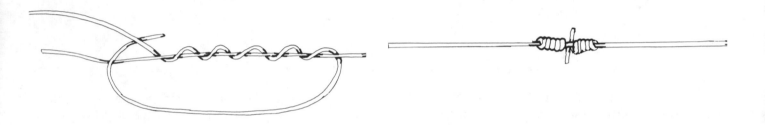

The blood knot is a very easy knot to master and has several uses.

SPYDER HITCH

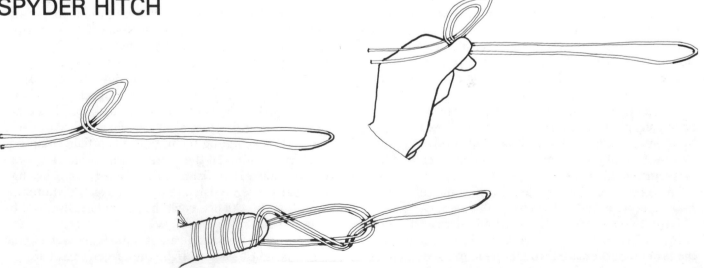

This knot is used to make a loop in the end of a line.

pull. Pull until the line breaks or you believe that you are close to breaking the rod. Do this with the various outfits you intend to use. Get the feel of these outfits. You will develop a second sense that will tell you when you are approaching that "fine line" of no return.

Try to remember that unless you are using extremely heavy gear you are not going to "stop them in their tracks." An albacore, tuna, yellowtail or other gamefish will usually make an extended run. The length of the run is determined by the size and strength of the fish, the manner in which the fish is hooked and tackle used. For example, a smallish bluefin tuna, hooked on 12-pound test line and a number 8 hook in the corner of the jaw, will doubtless make a run in excess of 100 yards. That same fish hooked on 50-pound test line, trolling, with an 8/0 siwash hook through the upper jaw will put up almost no fight.

When a hooked fish starts the first run, apply enough pressure to make it earn every yard of line off the reel. The fish should pull the line off the reel smoothly. If the rod is bouncing, the drag is too tight. Remember that as the line is pulled off the reel, the spool diameter decreases and thereby automatically increases the drag pressure. As the spool diameter decreases, drag setting must be reduced. For beginning anglers, this seems hard to remember, and I see many fish broken off because the angler will not back off on the drag as the line seems to be disappearing off the reel. I reality, this is not decreasing the drag tension, it is merely maintaining it.

Once the fish is stopped, it must be worked back to the boat. Here is where the experienced angler really shows his skill. Drag adjustment has to be made constantly as line is picked up or lost, keeping just inside the "fine line"—tight enough to gain line and yet light enough to allow the fish to run if it so chooses.

Here are some tips I have found helpful in a fight with a tough fish. I fight with both hands and arms. I pull with my left arm on the foregrip of the rod and use the reel handle to pull with my right. Except on an extremely heavy fish, I rarely take my hand off the reel handle when fighting a fish. Since most of us have more strength in our right hands and arms than in our left, it makes good sense to use the strongest arm to do a lot of the pulling; and not taking the hand off the reel handle makes for a lot more speed in pumping a fish to the boat. While keeping the drag tight enough to gain line, and at the same time light enough for the fish to take line on a sudden run, it is sometimes hard to gain line and the temptation is to tighten the drag. Many times this will result in broken line. Here is the way to get that extra drag and still maintain the light drag needed. On the up stroke of the pumping cycle, lift the thumb of your left hand off the foregrip of the rod and put in on the

line. Depress your thumb until the line is in contact with the foregrip for extra pressure. If the fish runs, all you need do is lift the thumb. A little practice will have you doing this maneuver routinely.

Short pumping is the method a lot of knowledgeable fishermen use to get the fish in the boat quickly, and "quick" is what it's all about when the bite is on. Short pumping or "using the short stroke" requires a reasonably fast taper rod, and one that is not too long—say under 8 feet. It works this way. Once the fish is down, as opposed to being out on the surface, the object is to "keep his head up" and keep him coming toward the boat. By pumping in the conventional manner, that is, long sweeping pumping strokes, the fish is turned and lifted toward the surface on each stroke and, as the angler regains line onto the reel on the downstroke, the fish turns and is again pointed toward the bottom, necessitating the lifting and turning of the fish on the next stroke. By short pumping, the strokes are much shorter with the tip of the rod rarely going higher than the angler, and, at the top of the stroke the rod is lowered with pressure maintained on the fish as the reel handle is turned to regain line. The object—the fish is not allowed to turn over and get his head down. Speed of pumping and constant pressure are the two keys to using this method successfully. Most "sharpies" combine the thumb pressure on the line, the short stroke and turning the reel handle as rapidly as possible on the downstroke. A high speed reel is a big help in this style of fishing.

Always remember that when the fish is finally close to the boat it is one of the most critical times of the fight. The main reason is that at this point the stretch factor of the line is at its minimum; the reel is full, and the fish will be maneuvering at close quarters. A great many fish are lost at the gaff. When getting close to the gaff, loosen the drag and rely on thumb pressure on the line. Be ready to move with the fish—up or down the rail of the boat. Be prepared to extend your rod over the side or under the boat is the fish moves that way. Listen for the instructions your crewman gives you. Always stand close to the rail, for to back away invites the fish to cut the line on the hull of the boat or the propellers and rudders.

If using a harness (and for bigger fish on long-range trips a harness is a necessity), always unsnap the harness when the fish is close to the boat as it is impossible to get the rod over the side in the event the fish goes under the boat if you are snapped into the harness. *This is important!*

Once the fish is gaffed, kick the reel out of gear and hold your thumb on the spool—hooked fish sometimes get off the gaff.

When fighting a fish from a dead boat (as you will do on most open-party sportfishers), you are at the mercy of the fish; you must move with the fish as the fight progresses. In this manner, the fish has some decided advantages. The most obvious is that the fish can fight you from the position it chooses, rather than the one you might prefer; and, if there is wind (which is generally the case), you will be fighting the drift of the boat, with the wind, as well as the fish; and you will usually find at the finish of the contest, you are fighting the fish upwind from the boat.

If you are fighting a large fish from a small boat, (one that follows the fish), you can force the fish to fight your game, rather than his. One of the best suggestions I can make is to fight the fish off to one side (on the same side all of the time), thus making the fish use the muscles on one side of the body, as opposed to both sides if you fight directly behind and away from the fish. Most anglers choose to merely follow the fish, waiting for it to tire. I prefer to work the fish at about a 45 degree angle from the bow off the same side of the boat during the entire fight, if possible. This sometimes requires some smart boat handling, and not all fish will oblige.

There have been some epic battles with moderate sized fish. My elder son, Steve, successfully fought a 26 pound bluefin tuna from our 22 foot Aquasport for 2 hours and 45 minutes on a 12-pound line. Steve is an accomplished angler and has taken many fine fish including marlin and sailfish. He claims he never had a tougher fish. Bill Nott of SAC (Sportfishing Association of California) was involved with a marlin that would not quit. His son (also named Steve) hooked a marlin at Catalina Island at about noon and they did not boat the fish until almost 9 p.m. – a fight of over 8½ hours! The fish was caught on 40-pound test line by an experienced angler with a fine boat and crew, and weighed only 150 pounds. There is no explaining this type of behavior – it just happens! My Dad, J. Charles Davis, II, tells of his 13½ hour fight with a Southern California broadbill in his book *Southern California Sportfishing*.

The toughest fight I ever had with a fish occurred at Roca Partida of the Revillegigedo Islands of Mexico. Although I have taken larger yellowfin tuna both at these islands and at Cocos Island off Costa Rica, this particular fish, which weighed 127 pounds was exceptionally strong and took about three hours to subdue on a 50-pound line. An angler can learn quite a bit about a fish during a fight of this duration.

All of the tuna have a noteworthy characteristic when being fought on hook and line. During the fight, if the fish shakes its head (which is transmitted to the rod as a series of short, sharp jerks), you can be assured that it is about to make another run. Make sure the drag will allow it.

When fighting a marlin or sailfish, if the line starts to rise to the surface, the fish is probably going to start jumping. Back off on the drag and be prepared for the acrobatics.

When fishing for yellowtail close to rocks or kelp, these fish will take advantage of these obstacles to cut you off or wrap the line and break free. Sometimes, but not always, you can turn the fish by throwing the reel out of gear and letting the fish run. Sometimes the fish will turn and run out to sea and can then be fought in the conventional manner.

Tangles are bound to occur when fishing on a crowded sportfisher. If you are involved in a tangle with your hooked fish, back off on the drag and ask for crew assistance. If there is more than one hooked fish involved in the tangle, remember that monofilament line cannot stand much heat. If one fish in the tangle is running against the stationary line of another, the running fish will always cut off the stationary one. Try to make sure that your fish is taking line slowly, so that cannot happen to you and so that you are not cutting off the other fellow's fish.

Kelp or calico bass are fished right in the kelp beds, many times. A hooked bass will often run into the kelp. Slack line will almost always get the fish moving so that it can be fought free. Many times it will be necessary to drop slack to the fish a number of times before the fish swims free of the kelp.

When fishing tuna or albacore and your line suddenly goes slack with a hooked fish, wind as fast as you can. The chances are that the fish is running at you.

Fishing barracuda with a monofilament line is sometimes the only way you can hook them. The sharp teeth of these fish make it very difficult to land them on mono, however. Try to set the hook as quickly as possible as opposed to when fishing with wire so that the shank of the hook will be on the outside of the jaw. Then back way way off on the drag and just turn the handle to gain line. Do not try to pump the fish. When the fish shakes its head, it is going to make a run, let it, when it is exhausted, it can be led to the gaff.

When fighting a tuna, and you get the fish to the boat, you will have the option of turning the fish over at the top of the circle, or letting the fish complete another circle. Always let the fish complete the circle, as pulling the fish over on the opposite side will many times dislodge the hook. I've done it several times.

When fishing for halibut, never lift the fish's head out of the water. Halibut open their mouths, flare their gills, shake their heads and *back up* when their heads are lifted from the water. Many times this results in the shaking of the hook. Halibut should be subdued with a club before removing from the gaff since they have been known to jump over the side.

14

HAYWIRE TWIST

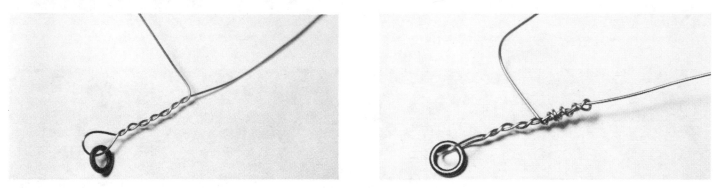

Bring the wire through the eye of the hook or swivel and bend into a loop. The two resulting wires are twisted against each other to form a series of "X's".

WIRE RIGGING

1

2

Two sleeves are slid onto the wire and a loop is formed with a simple overhand knot.

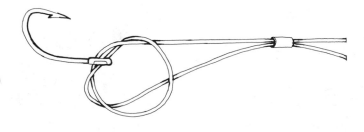

3

Pass the tag end of the wire through the loop a second time.

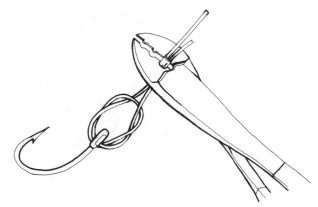

4

Slide the crimping sleeves down over the tag end and crimp.

Offshore trolling is the primary method of locating schools of albacore and tuna as well as a popular procedure for marlin fishing off the West Coast.

A good method of trolling—best for setting the hook.

"Schools of albacore are attracted to the boat and propwash."

Chapter 3
Trolling

Trolling is best divided into three categories: offshore, inshore, and surf and bay trolling.

Offshore trolling is the primary method of locating schools of albacore and tuna as well as a popular procedure for marlin fishing off the West Coast. Albacore are one of the most sought after fish that visit our coastal waters and are prime trolling fish when water temperatures are favorable. Albacore are caught in temperatures ranging from 58 to 72 degrees. As long as water temperature remains below 68 degrees the fish seem to take trolled lures well, but at temperatures above that, trolling produces fewer and fewer strikes.

When trolling from a live bait sportfisher (a party boat), the skipper will usually insist that relatively heavy gear be used—a 4/0 or 6/0 reel filled with 50-pound mono is about right. The reason is that trolling only locates fish for the majority of passengers who are not trolling. Therefore, it is important to get the hooked fish to the boat as soon as possible, bringing the school along with it. If light gear is used, hooked fish will be able to take so much line that the school might not come to the boat.

I believe schools of albacore and other fish take a trolled lure because the boat and resulting propwash act as attractors to the surface. My reasoning is as follows: the fish are looking toward the surface for food. A tightly-packed school of bait fish blots out the light and appears as a dark spot to fish below. A school of bait fish being attacked by predator fish, like albacore, naturally runs away from the attacker and is assaulted at the trailing edge of the school, with resulting white water as rampaging fish tear into the school. Straggler bait fish are picked off in the roiling

water. Now, picture the boat with trolling lines out. To fish below, this is a large area of blocked-out light—a dark spot not unlike the school of bait fish described earlier. At the trailing end of this fastmoving dark spot there is considerable white water in the form of propwash and wake. The boat's lures are traveling through this disturbed water. When albacore come up to see what all of the commotion is about—expecting some straggling bait fish—they are instead confronted with the trolled lures. If the color and size are right, they strike.

On large party boats it is not uncommon to troll as many as 10 lines at a time. In this case the crew may help regulate line length to prevent them from tangling and forestall some overanxious anglers from trolling too far back (some fishermen think that the farthest line out will be the first ones hit.) On private boats, even the small ones, it is possible to troll as many as five lines. It is not at all uncommon for the lines closest to the boat to be hit first. On private boats it is possible to use lighter lines and enjoy troll fishing to a greater degree—20- to 30-pound test line is adequate for these fish. Use monofilament straight to the lure, since albacore do not have teeth of line-cutting sharpness.

For many years the accepted albacore trolling lure was the "Jap Feather"—a simple lead head, usually chrome-plated, with ruby glass eyes and a hole through the center. Feathers of various colors were tied onto it. The preferred colors were white, red and white, blue and white, green and yellow, and black. In time, various other types of heads were designed: abalone inlaid, various colors of plastic, and the so-

Rock Cod outfit, showing extension reel handle and "rail board" or "rock cod plate", ahead of foregrip.

called "pearl head" made of shell – but still tied with feathers. A few years ago a new albacore jig appeared on the scene. It was called the "Hex Head," a lure with a chrome-plated hexagonal head and skirts of vinyl plastic instead of feathers. These lures met with immediate success. The most popular size weighs 2½ ounces. The skirts hold color better than dyed feathers (which had a tendency to run when wet) and vinyl colors are much more vivid. The West Coast commercial fleet uses these lures almost exclusively. They rig them with barbless double hooks since they pull the fish while running. Sport anglers use either a double barbed hook or a large single hook. I prefer the Mustad number 9510XXX in size 7/0.

Selecting a color is always a problem. If you are fishing with someone who was out the day before, always ask what color was "hot." If not, here's a guide that makers of the Hex Head have discovered after several years of experimentation: early in the morning – from gray dawn until full light – the best colors are black and, what they call the "super lure" which is a light-retaining, glow-in-the-dark green, and purple. As light intensity increases, green and yellow normally predominate as the best color combination. When the sun is well up, and on clear days, the better colors are red and white or blue and white. Sometimes at mid-day, when fish are not feeding, all-white or yellow and white jigs work best. In the late afternoon, the green and yellow again gets good and, as darkness approaches, the black, "super lure" and purple again take over.

Two of Carl Newell's high speed reels.

Hex head lures—the west coast commercial fleet uses these lures almost exclusively for albacore.

There is some controversy concerning the value of sinkers ahead of the lure. I believe sinkers are not necessary and are, in fact, a hinderance. At speeds normal for albacore—6 to 10 knots—any sinker that can be trolled on a rod and reel will do very little to keep a lure down, and I've never found a sinker that did not wobble at these speeds. Commercial trollers use 2- to 6-pound weights effectively, but these are too heavy for rod and reel use.

Reel drag should be set just under your line's breaking strength, when pulled from the tip of the rod.

The same techniques used for albacore work for tuna. Yellowfin tuna seem to prefer brighter colors, such as red and yellow, while bluefin tuna like all-white or blue and white. On long-range trips these same methods work for yellowtail, wahoo and other tropical species. But, in the waters of Baja and tropical offshore islands, wire leaders are a must. Wahoo and large yellowfin tuna will sever monofilament with their teeth. Wahoo hit lures within 20 feet of the transom as well as those trolled well back. In fact, they seem to prefer lures trolled right in the white water of the prop wash and wake.

For many years the only accepted method of marlin fishing in Southern California was to troll a dead flying fish, using an outrigger. The boat was stopped when a fish hit, allowing time for the marlin to swallow the bait before putting both the reel and boat in gear to strike the fish. This still works, but more and more fish are being taken each year with artificial lures—a very different method of trolling. As many as five lines may be used, including two from the outriggers. When a fish hits the trolled lure, boat speed is increased and several hundred yards of line are run out to insure that the fish is well hooked. The boat is then brought around in a gradual turn so the angler can start regaining line.

Many successful artificial lures have been developed over the past few years, the newest, CLONE lures are extremely effective, since they simulate various bait-fish patterns and colors. Most of these lures utilize brightly-colored plastic skirts, colored glass beads and other attractors behind a metal or plastic head, or a plastic scoop-nosed plug in combination with plastic skirts. Because marlin have a very bony head and mouth, sharp hooks are a must. Most manufacturers of these lures sharpen their hooks to a needle point. the effects of a day's trolling necessitates a sharpening prior to each use. I carry a small triangular file in my kit for this purpose.

Inshore trolling is effective for barracuda, bass, bonito and, at times, for yellowtail. Swimming plugs like "Rebels," and "Rapalas" work well for all of the species when trolled at a moderate speed. All-silver, mackeral bait lures, and the blue and white combinations are usually best when fish are feeding on small fish. In those years of pelagic red crabs, called tuna crabs, bright red lures are effective. A green and yellow combination is also good, because it approximates the colors of saury and smelt.

Light lines, up to 20-pound test, are the rule for this type of fishing, usually done from private boats.

Other good inshore trolling lures include aluminum jigs made in Southern California by a number of different manufacturers. These are the "Tady," "Salas," and others. Jigs come in an almost endless variety of colors and most of them work some of the time. Chrome, white, blue and white, and green and yellow are good basic colors. There are also several spoon-type lures that will catch fish. Among these are the "Spoofer," "Tady," "Krockadile," "Eppinger's Kop-E-Cat," etc. Chrome seems to be the best in this group. The small Japanese "Bonito Jig" is also effective in the normal colors of red and white, green and yellow, and blue and white. Best trolling is early moring and late afternoon.

Fishing for bass is best along edges of kelp beds and against rock walls, breakwaters and jetties. Barracuda and bonito are also found just outside large kelp beds along the coast and islands. Watch for bait and breaking fish on the surface. Let diving birds locate fish for you. It is possible to catch fish by trolling around the outside of anchored party boats, but etiquette demands you keep well clear of their lines. Remember that a good caster can throw a 4- or 5-ounce jig 100

yards! It is also poor policy to troll between an anchored boat and the kelp bed it is fishing. This will sometimes put down a school of fish that have been chummed out of the kelp.

Surf and bay trolling is really is really a lot of fun. Here is where you can use very light tackle—even your fresh water gear—and catch some good fish. There are a number of harbors and bays that produce good fishing for bass and halibut while trolling. For bass, diving plugs such as the "Bomber" are very good, as are feather jigs in green and yellow and red and white. Calico bass, sand bass and the spotted bay bass all hit lures well. It may take some experimenting to find the proper combination of lure, speed and color but, once found, fishing can be fantastic. These are fine eating fish, but remember, all of these fish have size limits, which should be observed.

A fact not well known is that halibut will take trolled lures kept right on the bottom. "Spoon Plugs" and "Russell Lures" are most effective because they stay down. In the bays, look until you find sand bottom, not mud. In the surf, troll just outside the breaker line with one eye cocked to sea—those big waves can sneak up on you. The lure should actually be plowing a furrow in the sand to be really effective, and slow trolling is the name of the game.

When using freshwater plugs, be sure to wash them off at the end of the day *in freshwater*. Many hooks and finishes used on this type lure will not take salt water well. It is also wise to be very careful when taking a fish off sharp treble hooks. I've had to remove several of these from my own as well as other people's hands. No fun at all.

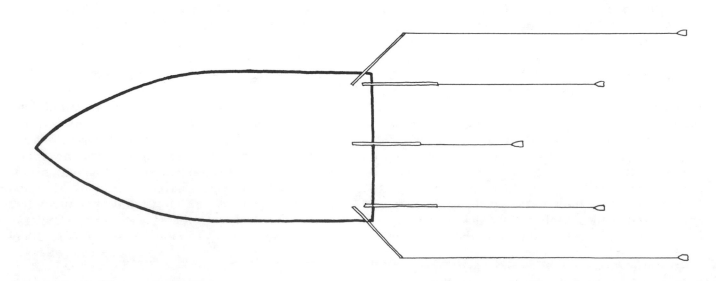

On private boats, even small ones, it is possible to troll as many as five lines.

*"...these boats have brought fishing for exotic tropical
species within wallet range of the average angler."*

Chapter 4
Sportfishing Boats

Boats developed for sportfishing in Southern California waters differ from those found in other areas. The most prominent feature is the large "bait tank" located on the after deck. This tank (or tanks) is a large box which carries thousands of baits for each day's fishing. Baits are kept alive by circulating a fresh supply of sea water through the tank, thus suppling plenty of oxygen.

Most boats now in operation are designed for passenger comfort. Local all-day and half-day boats (daylight hours only) have galley service where hot sandwiches and cold drinks are available. Boats in the offshore trade usually leave in the middle of the night and are sometimes at sea for two weeks or more on long range trips. These boats have super-excellent accommodations. Galleys on many of them would do justice to a fine restaurant: hot plates, chargrills and ovens are located alongside freezers, refrigerators and ice cube machines. Staterooms feature individual air conditioning, wash basins with hot and cold running water, foam-mattress bunks and showers. They are equipped with water-makers that convert sea water into fresh to supply all the water needs for long-range activities. Boats range from a length of 60 feet to well over 100 feet.

During hot runs of fish, boats may be filled to capacity with eager anglers, creating problems for those accustomed to fishing on boats with only a few friends. A big sportfisher may carry in excess of 80 passengers when the yellowtail or albacore are hitting well. Various systems are employed for assigning fishing space at the rail, but nearly all of the boats "rotate" their fishermen so that everyone has an

opportunity to fish the most desirable areas. Usually, the after area (the stern quarter) provides the best fishing and, naturally, that's where everyone wants to fish. The usual means of making sure that everyone is treated fairly is to rotate passengers every hour or so throughout the day in order to give everyone a "shot" at the stern. On many boats the bow is "open"— that is, there are no spots specifically designated and anyone may fish there. This is often one of the best fishing spots, except when trolling.

These boats are a far cry from the sportfishers of the 20's and 30's. The earliest passenger sportfishers I fished on were converted commercial fishing boats, water taxis and tugs. There was seldom a galley and almost never any bunks. Passengers sat or stood on deck during the slow trip to the fishing grounds and were many times soaked by spray. The fishing made it all seem worthwhile, but today's splendid boats make travel time a pleasant experience. With salons for leisurely dining, card games or visiting; bunks and staterooms assuring the angler of a comfortable place to rest while coming and going, it is no wonder that long-range trips have become so popular in recent years. Best of all, these boats have brought fishing for exotic tropical species within wallet range of the average angler.

Trips range from a few days to over two weeks and extend down the Baja California coast, up into the Gulf of California and across to the Mexican offshore islands. Prices for these trips are moderate, considering that all food, lodging and bait is provided as well as freezing the angler's catch. All boats regularly undergo standard Coast Guard inspection and must

A typical "local" sportfishing boat.

meet rigid licensing requirements. Modern navigation and communication electronics are employed as well as various types of "fish locators." Most boats have radar, loran, omega, automatic direction finders, VHF radio, single sideband radio and citizen's band radio as well as sonar units for the utmost in both safety and fish finding capability. Skippers and crews of these boats are exceptionally competent. They are in the sportfishing business because they love the sea and they love to fish. They work hard for moderate wages.

Long-range trips are sold by the day, and you can select a voyage of from five to 16 days. In five days you can fish Guadalupe Island or the coast as far as Geronimo Island, Sacramento reef, Benitos and Cedros Islands. The seven-day trip will take you on down the coast below Cedros Island or to Alijos Rocks. Longer trips extend down the Baja Peninsula and around the corner into the Sea of Cortez.

If you are fortunate enough to have time for a 14- or 16-day trip you will experience some of the most exciting fishing in the world today, near the Revillagigedo Islands. This is a group of four islands owned by Mexico, the closest of which, San Benedicto,

lies approximately 250 miles southwest of the tip of Lower California. They are on the same parallel as the lower tip of the big island of Hawaii and the south tip of Cuba, where water temperature ranges from the mid-70's to the mid-80's. The group includes San Benedicto, about 220 miles from Cape San Lucas; Socorro, 27 miles south of San Benedicto; Roca Partida, 60 miles west of Socorro; and Clarion, which is 153 miles west of Roca Partida. Socorro and Clarion are the only populated islands occupied by a small Mexican military contingents. San Benedicto is of recent volcanic makeup with the last recorded eruption in 1952. Steam was rising from the Volcano's main cone at the time of my most recent visit.

As the islands lie in the Eastern Pacific hurricane belt, sportfishing vessels usually fish only December through March. Only a relative handful of fishermen go there each year and the fishing is fantastic! On a 14-day trip, recently, 20 anglers caught over 400 wahoo, some weighing 80 pounds; almost 300 yellowfin tuna, up to 215 pounds; and assorted jacks, dolphin, grouper, etc. Three world record yellowfin tuna have come from Socorro and San Benedicto.

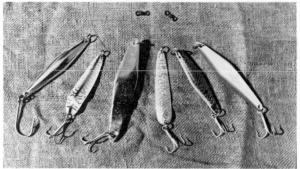

On long-range trips, it is wise to have a wide assortment of casting and yo-yo jigs along. The greatest number of jigs should be in chrome or polished aluminum, while blue and white, and green and yellow are also good. [top]

When the long-range boats get into areas of big yellowfin and billfish, light tackle has to be put in the rack and heaver rigs broken out. [left]

An assortment of trolling lures should be carried on long-range trips—these are by Sevenstrand. [bottom]

Boats developed for sportfishing in Southern California differ from those found in other areas. The most prominent feature is the large "bait tank" located on the after deck which carries thousands of live baits for each day's fishing.

There is a lot of good fishing from and around jetties and breakwaters, as well as in various bays of Southern California. Here a group of anglers fish near an offshore rig.

Steve Carlton and Steve Davis with a good catch of breakwater opal eye.

Steve Davis fishing the rock at Point Vincente.

25

Yellowfin weighing 50 or 60 pounds are easy to identify. They are a typical tuna with bright yellow fins and finlets. The pectoral fin is always longer than the distance from the tip of the lower jaw to the back edge of the gill plate. Owen Brown caught this 62 lb. yellowfin near Alijos Rocks, Baja California while aboard the "Qualifier 105."

Albacore are members of the same family as yellowfin and bluefin tuna and look much like these fish except for the obvious difference in the pectoral fins. Note the tag behind the second dorsalfin.

The Big Eye Tuna.

Whitebelly Rock Fish—also called "chucklehead"

White Fish

Yellowtail Rock Fish

Boccacio—the most abundant of the Rock Fish species

Bronze Spotted Rock Fish

Blue Rock Fish

Sculpin

Mexican Rock Fish

Wahoo action at Clarion Island aboard the "Polaris Deluxe."

Halibut put up a surprising fight—particularly if caught in shallow water. On the other hand, a fish may come to the boat with no fight whatsoever. But, beware of the one that doesn't fight! Halibut are notorious for throwing the hook at the boat. Roy Woolbright caught these two halibut from the Seal Beach barge.

Bait

Many of us take live bait for granted. We get on a sportfishing boat, the boat stops at the receiver or bait boat and picks up bait, and we are on our way to the fishing grounds.

Today, the live bait industry is big business, with large capital investments in nets, boats, light plants and receivers. Bait is almost always available, but wasn't always so. When I was a young man just starting out in the sportfishing business, it was common for sportfishing boats to return to the dock and refund the passengers for lack of bait. In most cases there simply was no bait available to the bait haulers, or haulers had deserted the landings to chase albacore during the height of the season.

All that has changed. In the past, small commercial fishing boats were converted to bait haulers. Today, specially designed, modern boats are equipped with mechanical net pullers, sonar, radar and other navigational aids. In some areas, bait is attracted to lights on small boats anchored in prime bait areas, then netted. Other boats haul bait on the open sea by locating schools of bait with sonar or setting at night on "balls of fire" – the phosphorescent shine of the fish.

The bait, primarily anchovies, is transferred to large holding tanks, or wells, on the baitboat and then transferred into receivers for storage. Anchovies are not strong, and require careful handling if they are to furnish prime bait.

For long-range trips, bait is "cured" after being caught by allowing it to remain in the receiver for several weeks prior to the trip. These baits are usually very strong and hardy as opposed to baits caught and handled shortly before use.

As this is being written, anchovy stocks off the Southern California coast are being threatened by commercial exploitation for use as fish meal and oil. It behooves every interested angler to acquaint himself with this problem and to communicate his beliefs to his Fish and Game Commission and the Fish and Game Department of the State of California.

What to Take On a Live Bait Boat

1. **Conventional rod with Newell 229F reel or equivalent. One spool full of 20- or 25-pound line. Rod of 6½ or 7 feet, with light tip.**

2. **If carrying a second outfit, a lighter rod, conventional or spinning, with 12- or 15-pound test monofilament. Rod may be 6 to 7 feet with a light tip.**

3. **If carrying a third outfit, a jigging outfit with a rod of 7 to 8 feet, stiff action, and a Newell 226F reel, or equivalent, with 40 or 50 pound monofilament line and aluminum spool.**

4. **Assorted hooks of the Wright and McGill style 318 or Mustad style, 94151, sizes 2/0, 1, 2, 4, and 6. Always check with the tackle store in the landing office as to what size you should be carrying. Special baits cause special sizes to be needed.**

5. **Assorted rubbercore sinkers, from 1/8 ounce through 1 ounce. These usually come in plastic bags holding several of the same size.**

6. **A few chromed ringed sinkers in 1 ounce, 1½ ounce and 2 ounces.**

7. **A few "Handy Dandy" or "Lucky Joe" snag gangs for bait fishing. Also squid jigs.**

8. **At least one rock cod gangion and a two pound sinker to go with it.**

9. **A good pair of long nose pliers with cutter blades, in a belt sheath.**

10. **One nail cutter type set of clippers.**

11. **A few Clout or Scampi style twin tailed leadhead jigs in various colors.**

12. **An assortment of "Candy Bar" type jigs. Tady, Salas, etc. [White, blue and white and chrome are the most popular colors, check with landing as to which colors are hot.]**

13. **Shorty rubber boots. [There are boots on the market for about $10.95, rubber or vinyl, and also some very fine rubber boots with non-skid soles for a good bit more money.**

14. **A hat.**

15. **Sunburn lotion if fair skinned.**

16. **Motion sickness remedy, if susceptible to seasickness.**

17. **Rod belt socket [butt rest].**

18. **Camera and lots of film.**

Sportfishing Piers, Landings and Harbors

Map No.	Facility	Day Boats	Charter Boats	Barge	Pier/Fishing Float	Small Boat Hoist	Launch Ramp	Small Boat Rentals	Bait/Tackle Shop	Restaurant	Live Bait Sales
1.	Gaviota				●	●					
2.	Goleta Beach				●				●	●	
3.	Sea Landing Cabrillo & Bass Sts., Santa Barbara, CA 93105 (805) 963-3564	●	●		●		●		●	●	●
4.	Ventura Sportfishing Landing 1500 Anchors Wy, Ventura, CA 93003 (805) 644-7363	●	●		●		●	●	●	●	●
5.	Channel Island Sportfishing 3285 Pelican Wy, Oxnard, CA 93030 (805) 985-8511 or (213) 457-9221	●	●				●	●	●	●	●
6.	Port Hueneme Sportfishing Port Hueneme, CA 93041 (805) 488-2212	●	●						●		
7.	Paradise Cove Sportfishing 28128 Pac Cst Hwy, Malibu, CA 90265 (213) 457-2511	●	●		●	●		●	●	●	●
8.	Malibu Pier Sportfishing 23000 W. Pac Cst Hwy, Malibu, CA 90265 (213) 456-8030	●	●		●				●	●	●
9.	Santa Monica Sportfishing Pier, Santa Monica, CA 90401 (213) 395-4230	●			●			●	●	●	●
10.	Venice				●				●	●	
11.	Marina Del Rey Sportfishing Fisherman's Village, Marina Del Rey, CA 90291 (213) 822-3625	●	●		●		●		●		
12.	Manhattan Beach				●				●	●	
13.	Hermosa Beach				●				●	●	●
14.	Redondo Sportfishing 181 N Harbor Dr, Redondo Beach, CA 90277 (213) 372-2111	●	●	●	●	●	*	●	●	●	●
15.	San Pedro										
	Cabrillo Beach				●		●		●	●	
	22nd Street Landing 141 W 22nd St, San Pedro, CA 90731 (213) 832-8304	●	●						●	●	
	Ports of Call Sportfishing Berth 79, San Pedro, CA 90731 (213) 547-9916	●	●						●	●	
16.	Long Beach										
	Municipal Facilities - Boat launch, ft. of Golden Ave. & 2nd St. Alamitos Bay										
	Queen's Wharf Sportfishing Berth 55, Long Beach, CA 90802 (213) 432-8993	●	●						●	●	
	Belmont Pier Sportfishing Belmont Pier, Long Beach, CA 90802 (213) 434-6781	●		●	●				●	●	●
17.	Seal Beach Sportfishing Municipal Pier, Seal Beach, CA 90704 (213) 434-1374	●		●	●				●	●	●
18.	Huntington Beach				●				●	●	
19.	Newport Beach										
	Municipal Pier				●				●	●	●
	Dune's Park						●				
20.	Balboa										
	Muncipal Pier				●				●	●	
	Davey's Locker Balboa Pavillion, Balboa, CA 92661 (714) 673-1434	●	●		●			●	●	●	●
	Art's Landing 503 Edgewater, Balboa, CA 92661 (714) 675-0550	●	●						●	●	
21.	Laguna Beach				●					●	
22.	Dana Wharf Sportfishing Dana Harbor, Dana Point, CA 92629 (714) 496-5794	●	●		●	●	●	●	●	●	●
23.	San Clemente				●				●	●	
24.	Helgren's Oceanside Sportfishing Oceanside Harbor, Oceanside, CA 92054 (714) 722-2133	●	●		●			●	●	●	●
25.	Mission Bay										
	Municipal Facilities						●				
	Seaforth Landing 1717 Quivira Rd, San Diego, CA 92109 (714) 224-3383	●	●			●			●	●	●
	Islandia Sportfishing 1551 W Mission Bay Dr, San Diego, CA 92109 (714) 222-1164	●	●			●		●	●	●	●

* Proposed

Sportfishing Piers, Landings and Harbors

Map No.	Facility	Day Boats	Charter Boats	Barge	Pier/Fishing Float	Small Boat Hoist	Launch Ramp	Small Boat Rentals	Bait/Tackle Shop	Restaurant	Live Bait Sales
26.	San Diego										
	Shelter Island				●		●				●
	Fisherman's Landing 2838 Garrison St, San Diego, CA 92106 (714) 222-0391 or (213) 625-1421	●	●						●	●	
	Loma Sportfishing 1402 Scott St, San Diego, CA 92106 (714) 223-1627 or (213) 628-2375	●	●						●	●	
	H & M Landing 2903 Emerson St, San Diego, CA 92106 (714) 222-1144 or (213) 626-8005	●	●						●	●	
	Lee Palm's Longrange Sportfisher's Ft of Emerson St, San Diego, CA 92106 (714) 224-3857	Long range trips only									
27.	**Avalon Boat Stand** Municipal Pier, Avalon, Catalina Island (213) 510-0455				●			●	●	●	

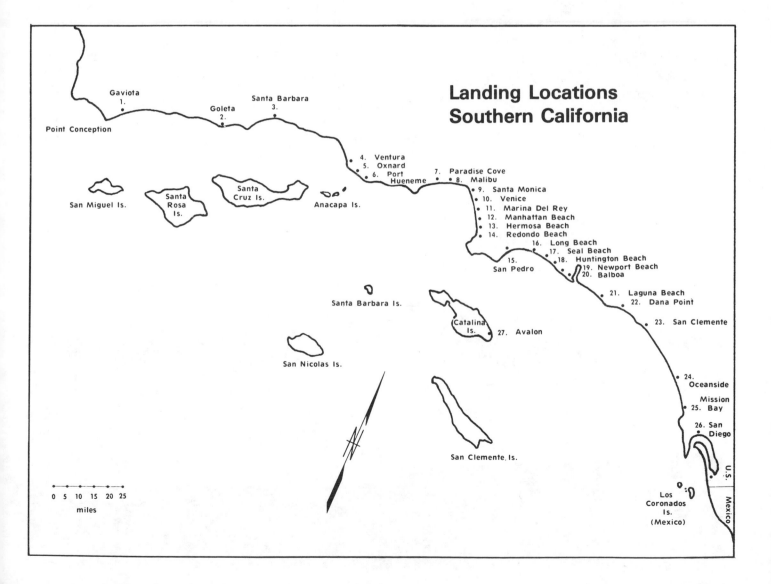

Landing Locations Southern California

Gaviota 1.
Goleta 2.
Santa Barbara 3.
Point Conception

4. Ventura
5. Oxnard
6. Port Hueneme
7. Paradise Cove
8. Malibu
9. Santa Monica
10. Venice
11. Marina Del Rey
12. Manhattan Beach
13. Hermosa Beach
14. Redondo Beach
15. San Pedro
16. Long Beach
17. Seal Beach
18. Huntington Beach
19. Newport Beach
20. Balboa
21. Laguna Beach
22. Dana Point
23. San Clemente
24. Oceanside
25. Mission Bay
26. San Diego
27. Avalon

San Miguel Is.
Santa Rosa Is.
Santa Cruz Is.
Anacapa Is.
Santa Barbara Is.
Catalina Is.
San Nicolas Is.
San Clemente Is.
Los Coronados Is. (Mexico)
U.S.
Mexico

0 5 10 15 20 25 miles

Binoculars

"Big eyes," as they are known by skippers and crew of the sportfishing boats, binoculars—or "glasses"—are a valuable aid in ocean fishing. Many times a pair of glasses has meant the difference between getting skunked and a good catch of fish for my passengers and me.

Glasses will reveal the presence of breaking fish, of birds, of bait and finning billfish that are invisible to the naked eye. It takes some practice to get used to looking through binoculars from a rolling or pitching boat but the results make it well worth while.

Over the years I have found that good quality 7 x 50 glasses are the best for boat use. My preference is the Bausch and Lomb war surplus glasses that were so plentiful right after World War II. They are hard to find now but do turn up in pawn shops and second-hand stores from time to fime. There are a number of excellent brands of 7 x 50 glasses, from both Germany and Japan, available in most camera stores.

Glasses seem to cut through the haze that is prevalent on the ocean a great deal of the time, when the tell-tail flash of a diving bird will mean finding fish.

For the skipper, glasses are an aid to navigation, enabling him to identify shorelines and navigation markers far beyond the ability of the naked eye. I, personally, do not like to put to sea without a good pair of "big eyes."

Binoculars will reveal the presence of breaking fish, birds, bait, and finning fish that are invisible to the naked eye.

Most boats now in operation are designed for passenger comfort and have excellent accommodations.

Chumming with live anchovies.

Author's son Mark, with a nice yellowfin tuna.

". . .expect albacore to make another run
just when you think you have them whipped."

Chapter 5
The Tunas

Albacore *[Thunnus alalunga]*

Albacore, the white meat tuna, are migratory fish that circle the North Pacific from the waters of Japan across to California, up the Pacific coast (depending on food and water temperatures) as far north as the Queen Charlotte Islands, British Columbia, and then across the Pacific and back to Japan. Young fish make as many as three migrations before reaching maturity, which is thought to be in excess of 50 pounds in weight; then spawn in an area some 600 miles north of the Hawaiian Islands and are presumed to die. The State of California conducted tagging experiments in the 1950's that authenticated this migration. Fish tagged during the study were recovered in various parts of this migration route, including the California area on the second trip around. Albacore are noteworthy not only for their long migration but also for the fact they grow so rapidly while traveling. Albacore travel in schools and usually when one is taken, more will be found in the same area.

Albacore are usually located by trolling various lures (hex heads, feather jigs, bone jigs) in water of 62 to 68 degrees. These fish may be located by bird activity, jumping bait, or breaking and jumping fish. Once albacore are located, live anchovies are chummed to attract fish within reach of bait cast by sportfishermen. A school of fish may "flash" under the boat for only a moment, hitting all baits in the water, only to disappear. Or, they might stay with the boat for hours, or even all day. Albacore caught in Southern California waters will weigh from 10 to over 40 pounds. Fish caught early in the season—late June or early July—are usually smaller fish, with the larger specimens appearing later in the year—sometimes as late as December.

A lively anchovy cast well away from the boat, either weightless or with a small rubbercore sinker, is the usual method for taking albacore. There is no need to let the fish run with the bait. Just point your rod at the fish and, when the line comes tight, set the hook. Be sure that the drag is preset for the line you are using, as your fish will probably run for 100 yards or more before stopping. Keep your fish directly in front of you at all times by following the direction it takes, even if this necessitates passing your rod around other anglers. Pump the fish to the boat, and then expect another run when you think you have him whipped. Albacore don't just roll over and play dead!

Albacore are members of the same family as yellowfin and bluefin tuna and look much like these fish except for obvious difference in pectoral fins. These fins are responsible for the nickname "longfin tuna." The fins extend in all cases to a length longer than the distance from the tip of the lower jaw to the back edge of the gill cover and, in larger fish, as much as half the total body length.

Recommended tackle falls into several classifications: a 4/0 or larger reel with 50-pound or heavier line or mono or dacron, and a sturdy trolling rod (most San Diego open-party sportfishing boats *do not* allow the use of dacron line for trolling). The rod should have a roller top and not exceed 7 feet in length. This rod is used for trolling and for those happy occasions when the albacore "eat the Paint off the boat" and it can be used with a heavy leader, large hook and small sinker to put fish into the boat in a hurry. A second outfit could be a 7½- to 8-foot medium-action rod for use with 40-pound line and a Newell size 344 reel with an aluminum spool and mono line. This equipment is suitable for a fairly hot bite but where necessary still to cast out from the boat. Finally, a light combination of 6- to 7-foot rod with a light tip but plenty of backbone (fast taper) for use with lighter line of 15- or 20-pound test mono. On this rod you may use a Penn 155 or 200, or—the author's favorite—the Newell 229F. This is the outfit to use when the albacore are "spooky" and, in order to get a strike, it is necessary to place a lively bait out and away from the boat.

Author and son Mark, with a pair of Socorro Yellowfin Tuna.

Top tips: If you see fish around the boat but cannot get a strike, try a smaller hook or lighter line – or both. You may have to drop down to a hook as small as a number 6, and line as light as 15-pound test. It takes a while, but big albacore can be landed on this gear.

Another tip: The best spot to fish for albacore, after the boat has stopped and is drifting, is the downwind corner of the stern. This is referred to as "the spot" by most skippers and deckhands. The wind will be at your back here, helping your cast, but the line will continually be drifting back to you as the boat drifts. Thumb the line in and be ready for a strike. This can be exasperating – constantly going to the bait tank for new bait (always change your bait after every cast) and then making another cast, but it pays off! If you observe commercial tuna and albacore boats, you will see that the fishing racks are on one corner; the corner they put downwind.

If the crew does not object, another good maneuver is to select the bait you wish to use with your left hand, then pick up two or three baits with your right hand. When you get back to the rail throw the baits with your right hand downwind as far as possible. By the time you have hooked on your bait and cast to the same spot, there is an excellent chance that there will be a hungry fish right there to take your bait.

If you have been in a successful stop (the local term for a period when the boat is stopped to fish) for some time, and things come to the point where there is only one hookup left going, the tendency is to stop fishing and go to the galley for a cold drink or take time to repair tackle. This is a mistake. *Every* time this happens – when the last hookup sees "color" – go to the bait tank, throw out a few anchovies and cast. Many, many times there will be one or more albacore rising to the surface with the hooked fish! The chum, and the splashing of the hooked fish on the surface will often cause them to feed.

At times, particularly at midday and in periods of warmer water – say, 69 to 72 degrees – albacore become very selective feeders. They will be seen swimming deep, just in sight, with pectoral fins outstretched to the sides. They will not come to the surface for chum and only occasionally take a bait. At these times there are several tricks that are well worth trying. First, try a long leader of light mono behind a small rubbercore sinker. If this doesn't work, try drifting a dead bait down to their level. To do this properly, you should hook the dead bait through the middle because a bait hooked in the head will sink head down – and dead baits don't sink that way. Finally, if nothing else works, look for a small, fat tom cod or herring. Hook the bait across the pelvic fins and drop it gently over the side. Since these baits are accustomed to living on the bottom, the chances are very good that your bait will take off in that direction – and an albacore just cannot stand the thought of one getting away.

When trolling for albacore, color is very important. The following guidelines for Southern California have proved to be very effective. (I emphasize Southern California because colors differ in various areas.) In the early morning, from gray dawn until full light, black, green and yellow, and the "glow-in-the-dark" green seem to be most productive. As light increases, black becomes less effective and the green and yellow predominates. At this point red and white, and in years of warmer water, red and yellow bring good results. On very bright days, toward midday, blue and white will be best with red and white a close second. During the middle of the day when jig strikes are few and far between, it will sometimes pay off to drop down in the size of the jig and change to very light colors such as all white or yellow and white. If you continue to fish during the afternoon feeding period, reverse the order from the moring routine and go from light to darker colors as the light fades. Purple, too, has recently become more popular.

Bluefin Tuna *[Thunnus thynnus]*
This fish initiated the sport of big game fishing. The first big game fishing clubs, The Tuna Club of Avalon and The Southern California Tuna Club were organiz-

ed around the turn of the century by sportsmen interested in capturing this great fish, popularly known as the "Leaping Tuna." In those days tuna weighing over 200 pounds were battled with the most primitive of boats and tackle. The fish were giants and so were the men who pursued them. In the beginning they fished with handlines. Then these early sportsmen laid down rules that have been the basis for all governed tournaments and the catching of record fish to this very day. We owe them our gratitude. Among the most famous of these early anglers was Dr. Charles Frederick Holder, founder of the Tuna Club.

The clubs remain—the oldest, The Tuna Club of Avalon, its weathered face to the sea, sits on tired old pilings in Avalon Bay on Catalina Island. The Southern California Tuna Club is headquartered at the Long Beach Marina. The clubs remain—but not the giant fish that inspired them. There has not been a bluefin tuna weighing over 100 pounds registered in either club since 1948.

The decline of these giant fish is no mystery. They are victims of the deadly purse seiner which was brought to California waters from the Mediterranean in the 1920's. Since bluefin tuna commonly school on the surface, they are easily seen by the "breeze" or dark spot they make. They also have a habit of jumping, for no apparent reason, which also betrays their presence. They are easy prey for seiners and, with the more sophisticated boats and their accompanying planes, the life of a bluefin tuna is relatively short.

These tuna follow a Pacific migration pattern which is similar to that of albacore. The tuna we catch usually appear in late May or early June and are available for most of the summer. They are so heavily fished that the size has diminished to a range of 10 to 25 pounds. Most fish caught from sportfishing boats are taken from the waters of Catalina Island or the Los Coronados Islands out of San Diego. These are fish that manage to elude the purse seiners and swim to the protected waters of these islands.

Many Southern California anglers believe bluefin tuna to be the most sporting of all fish which can be caught in our waters. They are selective feeders and very hook shy. It is not often that one is caught by accident. The angler who wants to catch a tuna must fish for him, and fish with the most threadlike line. A wisp of line, 12- or 15-pound test, is matched with a size 6, 8 or even 10 hook. A longer-than-average rod is used in order to get the bait well away from the boat. A light steelhead rod measuring 8 or 8½ feet makes a good tuna rod. A small Newell 220F or 229F reel completes the outfit.

To catch a bluefin tuna in the clear water of the islands is a great thrill, but the angler must take great pains to select only the finest anchovy for bait—one that has all its scales and the bronze-green color

Albacore are members of the same family as yellowfin and bluefin tuna and look much the same except for difference in the pectoral fins. Hex heads are top trolling lures for these fish.

characteristic of the liveliest of baits. After hooking the bait, ever so lightly behind the gill, it will take a long lobbed cast to land the bait softly. If you have chosen the bait well, delivered it correctly and have more than your share of luck, you will feel the bait become agitated as a tuna nears. If the line twitches, set the hook. No fish I know can sipt a bait more quickly than a tuna, and they inhale a small bait immediately.

Now the fun really begins! Tuna take line at a phenomenal speed once they decide on a direction. However, they have the habit of first making several short dashes – 10 yards to the right, then right at you, then another short dash to the side. This is usually followed by a heart-stopping run of 100 yards or more in one direction, usually right on the surface. It is not uncommon to have 100 yards of line out of the water while fighting one of these fish. Look out for gulls and pelicans coming in to get the chum. One touch of a wing and goodby tuna! You must fight the fish with a delicate hand. The light line and the small hooks do not allow for any mistakes. Too much pressure and the line lets go, or the small hook cuts its way out.

At times tuna will not take bait on the surface. They will boil and eat the chum being thrown by the deckhand – almost throwing water in your face – but will not touch a baited hook. Here's a trick that will usually produce a strike under these conditions. Using the same gear and bait, lob a cast out underhand or simply drop it over the side and let the bait swim freely. You may have to do this a number of times, changing bait each time, until you get one that will swim straight down. When you do, you will probably get a strike.

At times, bluefin tuna will be found offshore with albacore. Once in a while they will behave like albacore and bite everything in sight, but most of the time the opposite is true, and tuna will cause albacore to become selective. Then you'll have to use tuna tactics and tackle to catch either one.

The bluefin is distinctive in that it's steely blue on the back without any of the bronze or yellow of the yellowfin, and the pectoral fin is always shorter than the head. They are fine eating – fried, baked or canned – and are particularly sought after by many for use as sashimi (raw fish with soy and wasabi, or dry mustard).

Bluefin rarely hit lures but may be taken occasionally by trolling. An all white feather or skirted lure trolled at 8 to 10 knots is usually the most productive. It is not uncommon to see lots of jumping tuna in the Catalina Channel and not be able to get a strike. They seem to be jumping for the pure joy of jumping rather than chasing bait.

Very rarely bluefin tuna will take cast "iron" type jigs. These are occasions when they are found offshore in "meatballs" feeding on the surface.

Yellowfin tuna [Thunnus Albacores]

Yellowfin tuna are not often found in Southern California waters, but since they are a prime target on long-range trips, they are incuded in this book.

Yellowfin weighing 50 or 60 pounds are easy to identify. They are a typical tuna with bright yellow

Big eye tuna from Southern California waters.

Jerry Livoni, of Long Beach, with his 214 pound yellowfin tuna.

fins and finlets and the pectoral fine is always longer than the distance from the tip of the lower jaw to the back edge of the gill plate. The back of the fish, when alive, is a golden-bronze hue, and has distinct white spots on the belly, while alive.

Identification of larger specimens is difficult because the Pacific big-eyed tuna is very similar in appearance. Larger yellowfin develop a beautiful pair of sickle fins — the second dorsal and the anal fin. These larger fish with the distinguishing fins were, for a long time, considered a separate species and were called Allison tuna. Although the largest caught on rod and reel to date weighed just over 388 pounds, it is believed that yellowfin achieve a weight of over 500 pounds.

Large or small, the yellowfin is a great fighter. They strike trolled lures well and will come to the boat when chummed. The same techniques used for albacore work well with these close relatives, except that yellowfin will more often hit a cast lure from a dead boat than will albacore. Bright chrome jigs seem to work best.

Yellowfin do not migrate across the Pacific as do albacore and bluefin, but move north and south with favorable water temperatures and feed. They prefer much hotter water than albacore and are rarely found in water cooler than 72 degrees. When we do get yellowfin it is usually late in the albacore season. They

will sometimes mix with albacore, and many a fisherman, thinking he has hooked an albacore, has watched his line disappear as a big tuna took it all. Occassionally these heavy stray fish are landed in local waters — usually by someone who is trolling with a heavy rig. Most of the larger fish have proven to be bigeye tuna.

On long-range trips, yellowfin tuna are caught from the Cedros Islands all the way down the Baja Peninsula — at Alijos Rocks, sometimes at Guadalupe Island and, the best spot of all, the Revillagigedo Islands. These fish are unbelievably strong, stubborn fighters and it is not uncommon for an angler to be on one of these 100 pound fish for several hours.

On long-range trips, the common practice is for the angler to fight the fish from a standing position, without a chair, and follow the fish around the boat, not to follow the fish with the boat. This means that a harness is necessary and that the angler had better be in good shape, physically. Fifty-pound monofilament line is the minimum size I would recommend, on at least a 4/0 reel, preferably a 6/0 for the over 100-pounders. I have been "spooled" time after time on 4/0 reels and have had to resort to the more cumbersome 6/0 to land my fish. I did beat a 110-pounder at Guadalupe Island on a number 500 Jigmaster and 40-pound mono line in 1967 — but

The Tuna Club of Avalon, its weathered face to the sea, sits on tired old pilings in Avalon Bay on Catalina Island.

ruined the reel in the process. I landed another 100-pounder in 1972 at Soccorro on a Jigmaster and 50-pound mono but I had to fasten a back-up rig to that outfit, throw it over the side and fight the fish on the second rig for an hour before I landed that fish. They are tough! Most serious anglers bent upon catching large yellowfin tuna have found that the Penn International reels in size 50 or 50W are best, because of the superior drag system, and almost indestructable construction.

Yellowfin tuna are classed as "light meat tuna" and are second in value to albacore. The yellowfin is a heavily exploited fish by the large "superseiners". Extensive tagging has established the migration pattern as well as fishing pressure on these fish. In 1967, at Guadalupe Island, I was with a party on the boat "Tick-Tock" that tagged about a dozen yellowfin tuna weighing from 30 to 40 pounds each. Almost half these fish were recovered within six months by purse seiners operating 200 to 400 miles from the tagging location.

It has been learned that these tuna will strike a bright-colored trolled lure that makes a great surface commotion. Brilliant reds and yellows are a favorite color combination and plastic skirts of these colors, when fastened to scoop-nosed plugs that dive and splash, are effective attractors. Wire leaders are a suggested for fish weighing over 50 pounds, since, unlike albacore, large tuna have just enough teeth to cut even heavy-weight monofilament, although many long range anglers are now fishing large tuna by doubling the last few feet of their mono line, and then snelling a hook to the doubled line. The theory is that unwanted sharks will easily cut even the doubled mono, and the tuna seem more inclined to hit mono leaders than wire. A very large tuna can still chew through doubled mono, though.

Bigeye tuna *[Thunnus obesus]*

Until recently, bigeye tuna catches were rarities in Southern California waters, but during the years of 1979, 1980 and 1981, there were impressive catches of these fish made in both Southern California and Baja waters, including several world records. Over the years, a few bigeye have been reported from time to time, and occasionally some large yellowfin tuna. It now appears likely that almost all of the larger fish were in reality, bigeye. Yellowfin tuna and bigeye are closely related species, and are quite similar in appearance, except for a few characteristics. The body of the bigeye is quite compressed, hence the latin name, Thunnus obesus, or "fat tuna", which makes this fish appear stubbier and less streamlined than the yellowfin. Yellowfin have distinct white spots on the belly, which are missing on the bigeye, and the second dorsal and anal fins of large yellowfin generally elongate into beautiful crescents, while those of the bigeye remain short and stubby, no matter the size of the fish. Most bigeye taken locally the past few years have been of good size, 60 pounds and over, and many fish over 100 pounds were taken. Most have been taken trolling with either large "Clone" type lures in mackeral and goatfish patterns, or with large chromed "Hexhead" lures. If there is real question as to species, the sure fire method of identification requires an examination of the liver. Bigeye livers are striated, with light colored stripes radiating from the center of the lobes while yellowfin livers do not have such stripes. Bigeye are fine fighters, ranked right with the yellowfin, and are fine eating. I am now convinced, after re-examining the pictures of a 110 pound tuna I took at Guadalupe Island in 1967, that the fish we thought was a yellowfin, was in reality a bigeye.

Skipjack *[Katsuwonus Pelamis]*

Found worldwide in tropic seas, the skipjack only reach the Southern California fishing areas when we have abnormally high water temperatures—in the 70's. They are sometimes found mixed with both yellowfin tuna and albacore. They are voracious feeders. Very fast, the skipjack puts up an exciting fight, with short dashes and sizzling surface runs. Although these fish sometimes weigh 40 pounds, a 15-pounder is considered large in our waters.

In spite of the fact that the skipjack is one of the most important tuna to the commercial fishing industry (they are canned as grated tuna), they are not considered a good table fish.

Skipjack hit trolled lures well, preferring short lines in the white water. They have small teeth, so wire leaders are not required. They can be identified by lateral dusky stripes on the belly and their shape, which is much like a football. There are also some beautiful electric-blue markings on the back near the tail, visible on live fish.

"This rugged fish has been the mainstay of the San Diego sport fishery for years."

Chapter 6
Yellowtail

This rugged member of the jack family has been the mainstay of the San Diego sport fishery for years. They are common from well down in Mexico, including Cape San Lucas and the waters of the Gulf of California, to the Channel Islands of Southern California. In local waters, the average yellowtail weighs from 15 to 25 pounds, with an occasional larger fish being taken. They take a wide variety of baits, with squid, anchovy and the mackerel (both Jack and green) preferred.

Jigs are very effective on yellowtail, and are fished a number of different ways. Yo-yo jigging works well, but requires a reel with a fast retrieve and a strong pair of arms. It works this way: the jig, a 4- to 12-ounce "Candy Bar" type, is dropped to the bottom in 100 to 200 feet of water. All slack is taken up and the jig is lifted sharply off the bottom for 4 or 5 feet. This is repeated several times, following the jig back down with the rod as the fish sometimes takes the jig "on the sink." If there is no strike, the jig is retrieved as fast as possible, clear to the surface. Don't be afraid of reeling too fast—you can't! Some years ago a transmission was developed for the standard Penn reel which increased the gear ratio from about four-to-one to over 16-to-one, and yellowtail loved it. Be sure that the drag is tight enough to set the hooks, but light enough to let the fish run.

Perhaps the biggest thrill is casting a jig on the surface to boiling fish. Many times it is possible to see the fish take the jig. Lighter lures, weighing no more than 4 ounces, are used for surface jigging, and are usually tied directly to the mono. Sometimes, however, a short length of wire (12 or 14 inches in length) is used to improve jig action. Check with deckhands or the landing tackle store concerning the size and color jig that is currently most productive. At time, jigs work more effectively if they are cast as far as possible and then allowed to settle part way, or all the way, to the bottom, before retrieving. Speed sould be varied until you find that which is best.

Live bait fishing produces by far the largest portion of the annual yellowtail catch. This fish is a cinch with live squid when it is available. Squid may either be fished deep, with sinkers, or flylined right on the surface when fish are visible. The angler can usually get away with fairly large hooks and line when using live squid—2/0 hooks and 30-pound monofilament is about right. I prefer to use a sliding sinker right down on the hook, and the squid should be hooked through the tip of the tail. The most productive method when using a sinker is to cast the squid and allow the sinker to carry the bait to the bottom, thumbing the line on the way down. If it isn't hit on the way down, start retrieving with a pumping motion, giving the bait a stop-and-go action. Be prepared to throw the reel out of gear when a fish hits so there is time for the fish to swallow the bait—about three or four feet of run is usually sufficient—then, set the hook.

Fishing for yellowtail with jack mackerel can be very productive, but exasperating! This bait doen't run hard so you must just "soak" them in order to get a strike. They are best hooked across the nose, and the hook and line sizes are determined by how well fish are biting. In most cases it is possible to use fairly heavy line and large hooks with Spanish mackerel bait: 1/0 hooks or larger, and 25- or 30-pound test

The author and his son Mark with yellowtail caught at the Coronado Islands using live squid.

line. When a yellowtail picks up a bait, enough time should be allowed for the fish to get this larger-than-average bait well down. Mackerel have a rather tough head, making it more difficult to hook the "yellow." A rather stiff rod is necessary – 7 feet or longer – to set the hook. And, one must really set hard in order to get the hook through a Spanish mackerel and into the yellowtail.

Sometimes yellowtail are caught on green mackerel. It's puzzling how they eat baits this large. A 20-pound yellowtail will take a mackerel weighing well over a pound. When using green mackerel you'll need a line of 40- or 50-pound test and large hooks, 5/0, or larger. It is sometimes difficult to know when a fish has taken the bait because the mackerel pulls so hard. But, thumb your reel, and if you don't feel the quiver of the mackerel you can be fairly sure that the "yellow" has the bait. Give the fish some time to swallow this big bait – let it run 10 or 12 feet – then, set the hook, hard. Often, a yellowtail will return to a bait that has been pulled out of its mouth and hit it again. If you miss a strike, retrieve the bait fast with tip in the air and be prepared to throw the reel out of gear at the strike. It sometimes pays to clip a bit off both lobes of a mackerel's tail to slow it down.

When using anchovies it is usually necessary to drop down to light line and small hooks. A size 4 hook and a 20-pound line is the place to start – going lighter and smaller if you have to. Since the anchovy is not a strong bait, it cannot act natural with heavy gear. Yellowtail become very selective with anchovies and can annoy you with their boiling and swimming around the boat – "all show and no go!" It takes a good bait, well presented on light gear, to get a strike. And then you have to contend with the fact that, of all the fish we catch here, the yellowtail has the keenest instinct for using whatever hazard is available to beat you. What I mean is this: if you are fishing near kelp, that's where your fish will head, to hopelessly wrap your line. Or, if you're near a rocky reef, that will be the yellowtail's destination. If there is nothing else available, the anchor line will do. Some examples: yellowtail are often found far offshore under patches of floating kelp – "kelp paddies." In fact, there may well be a large school of fish under a relatively small paddy. These fish will usually hit well, taking either jigs or bait, but with hundreds of fathoms of water under the boat and only one small patch of kelp, that's invariably where your fish will go.

On an overnight albacore trip out of Long Beach we anchored, after the first day of fishing, in the middle of Pyramid Cove, San Clemente Island. We were in about 120 feet of water over a clear sand bottom. I was called about 4:00 a.m. for the watch and one of my duties was to remove dead anchovies from the bait tank. I scooped out several and dropped them over the stern. I then picked out a few more and returned to the stern where I saw a very large yellowtail, perhaps 60 pounds, swimming around picking up the dead baits I had discarded. I quickly got an outfit and, after several attempts, succeeded in hooking this beautiful fish – on a 30-pound line. I figured that the fish was too big, that he would beat me, but I was waiting to see how he would do it. Well, that fish stopped and flared out his gills, disgorging the baits he had eaten, shook his head and made a short run of about 10 yards out into the dark. Then, he turned and came by the stern and made another run of about the same distance on the other side. He stopped again and shook his head. Here we were – at least a quarter of a mile from any rock or kelp – so that fish swam right up under my feet and cut the line on the propellers. There was nothing I could do about it. Now, I know fish cannot reason – but that fish did something that came mighty close to it.

When we have an explosion of the bonito population they can get to be a real nuisance when trying to catch yellowtail, since bonito are faster and much more aggressive. A little-known fact is that you can catch yellowtail on a good-sized fillet off the bonito, and bonito will not touch it. On the long-range trips to Gaudalupe Island and other Baja hotspots, larger yellowtail are usually caught on slabs of yellowtail or bonito on the bottom. When nothing else works, a grunion or smelt will get a strike. Hook the smelt through the nose and cast as far as you can; then retrieve across the surface, reeling as fast as you can; with the tip held high. When a "yellow" takes a bait this way you don't have to throw the reel out of gear. Just drop the tip, swing, and you're on! I have also seen the time when the only way to hook yellowtail was with dead bait drifted down with other dead bait chum. This takes a small hook buried in the bait – and not many of the fish hooked in this manner are landed.

Incidentally, pompano, – sometimes found in the bait tank – are also good yellowtail bait.

". . .barracuda show the effects of overfishing and pollution."

Chapter 7
Barracuda

At one time the most popular sport fish in Southern California, the barracuda, shows the results of over-fishing and pollution. There is now a 28-inch size limit with the hope that this fish will stage a comeback. Barracuda are common from Point Conception to the Cedros Island area of Mexico. These fish may attain a weight of 12 pounds, although 10 pounds is considered very large. There average weight is 4 to 6 pounds.

Barracuda are excellent fighters for their size and strike both lures and bait readily. They react well to chum and can be held around a boat for hours. When they are in a feeding mood they will hit anything that moves. On the other hand, they can be very selective feeders. That's where the fun comes in! Barracuda can be enticed to strike even when they have a full gullet. They hit feather jigs, candy bar type lurs, spoons and who knows what? It often takes considerable experimentation to find the correct combination of size, color and speed but, once it's found, you can catch all the law allows.

Feather jigs are particularly deadly and are little used these days. Red and white, blue and white, yellow and green, and all-black are good colors for attracting these fish. They will hit on a slow, lazy retrieve with long sweeps of the rod, or with short, erratic movements. Many times they follow the jig or lure right to the boat before striking.

One of the most successful methods for catching barracuda is called "pump bait" fishing. Always remember in fishing barracuda with bait to use wire leaders as the fish have very sharp teeth and are seldom landed with straight mono. For "pump bait" fishing, place a chromed ring-sinker (weighing one or two ounces) about three feet ahead of your number one or two hook. Run the point through the anchovy's nose, coming through the lower jaw and out the top of the nose ahead of the eyes. Cast your bait out and allow it to sink to the bottom — you may even get a strike on the way down. If not, start your retrieve. Keep the rod tip high (at a 45 degree angle or higher) and reel down three or four turns of the handle, lowering rod at the same time; stop reeling and lift tip of rod to the upright position again — stop. Reel down again. Repeat this procedure until you have returned your bait to the surface. Change speed of the retrieve until you find the one that works best.

When a barracuda hits the bait you must simultaneously drop the tip and throw the reel out of gear! This takes practice and can be frustrating but the fish must be given time to swallow the bait (usually takes only a few feet). Then throw the reel back into gear and strike. Many times you will see fish follow the bait to the surface before taking it. Anchovies are the best — and almost only — bait for barracuda although they will occasionally take grunion or smelt.

Barracuda are fair eating but require care after they are caught. They should be laid flat in a damp sack out of the sun, if possible, since a dried-out, curled-up barracuda is not much good for anything. The roe of the female is excellent eating, and if you look carefully you'll find that barracuda are one of the few fish in which it is possible to determine sex before cleaning. The female has a charcoal black edge on the anal and pelvic fins; male fins are edged with yellow or olive.

Good lures for barracuda, beside the feather, are the Spoofer, Tady, Candy Bar and Salas. The Tady, Candy Bar and Salas are cast-aluminum jigs, and best colors are chrome, white and green, or yellow. The Spoofer is a spoon-type lure with waffle-like configuration at the tail, and works well in either chrome, or white with a red stripe. Tady also manufactures a metal-stamped spoon-type with a good barracuda action — chrome with green or blue work well. Then, there are the "old standbys," including the Streamline Dodger, the Hex-Bar Jig and the "S" Dodger. "Yo-yoing" these lures is usuaily the best bet.

Barracuda are excellent fighters for their size and strike both lures and bait readily.

Barracuda are fair eating but require care after they are caught.

Be careful when removing hooks, as a barracuda can very easily inflict nasty cuts with its prominent teeth.

Some very good barracuda fishing occurs in Santa Monica Bay early in the year, with fish showing up in late January and on into February and March. These are usually large fish, 7 to 9 pounds, and are caught offshore in the vicinity of Manhattan Beach and El Segundo. Many times they are located by "bird schools" that congregate as ravening barracuda drive schools of baitfish such as anchovies, to the surface. These are usually fast moving schools and it doesn't pay to anchor; just drift and cast to the breaking fish. They usually hit lures well when they are feeding on bait. When they quit hitting, look for another bunch of birds while slowly trolling lures in the area where fish were last seen. Some years provide good early season fishing for "log" barracuda (the term usually reserved for fish over 7 pounds) at a spot known as The Rock Pile, which is located down the Mexican Coast a short distance below Coronado Islands off of

San Diego. Many times these large schools of fish provide great angling during the months of March and April at this location. The greatest concentrations of barracuda usually occur during the months of May and June along the Southern California Coast, with good catches coming from the areas of La Jolla, Oceanside, Dana Point, the Huntington Beach Flats, the Horseshoe Kelp, Catalina Island, Rocky Point, Santa Monica Bay and the Deep Hole above Point Dume. At times, barracuda are also taken at San Clemente Island, at some of the Channel Islands and in the fall, sometimes at San Nicolas Island. They are sometimes taken down the Baja Peninsula on long range trips, but since they do not freeze well, they are not usually a target fish on these trips.

There are a number of barracuda which are members of the same family — both larger and smaller species are found in Mexican waters. Wherever I have encountered them, they appear to have the same fascination for lures. They are a fun fish, and are also excellent baits for swordfish and black seabass.

Bonito are one of the finest small game fish available to the inshore fisherman. Sportswriter Bob Whitaker of Phoenix lands one on a flyrod at King Harbor, Redondo.

"Sometimes called the 'poor man's tuna.'"

Chapter 8
Bonito

Sometimes called the "poor man's tuna," bonito are one of the finest small game fish available to the in-shore fisherman. This fish is a great one for learning the sport, for several reasons:

First, bonito are great fighters when taken on tackle suitable to their size. They weigh from a couple of pounds to over 12, and when taken on heavy fresh water or light salt water gear, they really give a good account of themselves. A 4 or 5-pound bonito on an 8 or 10-pound line and matching rod will take 10 or 15 minutes to subdue. Bonito fight much like their cousin, the bluefin tuna, with long runs on the surface and a circling, slugging fight under the boat before being landed.

Second, they are available. Bonito are found in many areas almost year-round. The warm water outfalls of electrical power plants seem to hold them at King Harbor in Redondo Beach and near the mouth of the San Gabriel river in Seal Beach. At a number of these locations the fishing is done inside the harbors and a rowboat is actually all that is needed to get to the fish.

Third, these fighters will hit a wide variety of lures and baits. On the other hand, they can be as selective as tuna. They like anchovies, but the bait must be free swimming and natural. Small hooks are the rule—6's and 8's. A collar-hooked anchovy made to jump on the surface with the rod tip will usually produce a strike if bonito are around. As with most predatory fish, set the hook immediately—just lower the tip and swing!

Although bonito have a mouthful of needle-pointed teeth, these are so spaced that wire leaders are not necessary. However, a pair of long-nosed pliers is a must for removing hooks.

At times these fish will hit lures very well—feather jigs, small, wobbling spoons of chrome and red, and flies are all effective. In fact, this is a top fish for the salt water fly-rodder, and King Harbor annually attracts fly fishing clubs from as far away as Phoenix, Arizona.

Bonito seem to be attracted by surface commotion and years ago people started using a "Bonito Splasher" to attract these fish. The first splashers I saw were net corks with a sinker in the center hole for weight. A short leader was attached behind the cork and then a feather jig. After as long a cast as possible, the cork was pulled through the water with a jerking motion which caused a bubbling, surface disturbance, as the feather dragged through the agitated water. This same system is still used today, with variations. Some anglers use a splasher in combination with a fly and very long leader—sometimes as long as 8 feet—for the educated and finicky feeders. Splashers are usually painted white, or red and white, and are wood. A rubber ball will also make an acceptable splasher. Spinners, too, are excellent bonito lures with white or yellow bodies preferred. The "Roostertail" in ½- or ⅜-ounce sizes has proved to be one of the best.

Bonito are not considered top grade table fare but they are excellent smoked and, if bled when caught and properly cared for, they are good barbecued or baked.

Besides being found at power plant outfalls, bonito are found along kelp beds, at the islands and, on occasion, mixed with barracuda and yellowtail. At times they can be pests. Because of their speed and voracious appetites, it is frequently impossible to get a bait through them to other fish.

This modest size black sea bass was caught off of Ascuncion Bay, Baja, Calif. Mexico, by the author.

"...there are indications halibut may stage a comeback."

Chapter 9
Inshore Species

Halibut *[Paralichthys californicus]*

The California halibut was at one time a very important member of the ocean sportfish family. Unfortunately, overfishing by both sport and commercial interests have left very few of these popular fish. There is now a size limit of 22 inches as well as a bag limit of five in Southern California, but there are indications these fish may stage a comeback.

Halibut in this area have attained a weight of over 50 pounds but today, a 10-pounder is considered a good fish. Halibut lie on the bottom, preferably in sand, and cover themselves by flipping sand over their bodies; then, with only eyes protruding, they await their prey.

The Halibut feed on any bait—alive or dead. Of the smaller fish, anchovies are preferred; herring, squid and tom cod are the desirable baits for larger fish.

The most successful fishing is in the spring, when halibut come in to spawn. Drifting across the sandy flats, outside a surf line, is the usual method of halibut fishing. The proper rig is a shiny sinker (just large enough to keep the bait on bottom), tied to the end of the line. Tie a dropper loop up about 10 inches, then attach a leader about 30 inches long—all of 20-pound monofilament. Hook sizes run from a number 4 for the small anchovy to the 4/0 for larger baits. The Siwash hook is considered best by most knowledgeable anglers—although some fishermen prefer a small treble hook. (See illustration)

Halibut fishing is an art. Unlike most fish, halibut do not swallow the bait immediately after the strike—and time *must* be allowed for the fish to swallow the bait. Since the boat is usually drifting, this can be difficult to manage. Halibut usually take the bait crosswise and will hold it for some time before swallowing.

Halibut put up a surprising fight—particularly if caught in shallow water. On the other hand, a fish may come to the boat with no fight whatsoever, apparently not awake from its lethargic existence on the bottom. But, beware of the one that doesn't fight! Do not lift any halibut's head out of the water prior to the gaff—especially the nonfighter! Halibut are notorious for throwing the hook at the boat. They are equally well known for jumping off the gaff or off the deck after having been landed. For a fish its size, halibut have awesome teeth, many fishermen have been fooled by its apparent somnolence only to suffer a nasty set of punctures when trying to remove a hook with fingers instead of pliers. *Don't try it!*

Believe it or not, halibut readily take lures. A white or yellow Marabou jig, dragged slowly across the bottom will sometimes work well, as do chrome Hex jigs, and clouts. The halibut is one of the best eating fish in local waters.

The story of how the halibut got its name is interesting. In England, in the early days, all flat fish were called "butts" and the best of the butts were saved for the priests, or holy men; thus the name.

Most serious halibut fishing is done by drifting. These fish rarely swim after food—they prefer to let the food come to them. Drifting accomplishes this by dragging baits across the bottom.

One of the most important keys to successful halibut fishing is keeping the bait on the bottom. This may sound very basic, but it is not nearly as simple as it seems. Wind and current move the boat at varying speeds, and the depth of the water may also change. All these factors affect the weight necessary to keep the bait right on bottom where these fish live. Remember, a sinker heavy enough to get your bait to the bottom may not necessarily be heavy enough to keep it there. Halibut will rarely come off bottom after a bait; they usually snap at it as it drifts by, then settle back down with the bait only partially in the mouth. The bait may be held this way for a minute or so before it is swallowed. Since the boat is drifting, you must fish in free spool, with light pressure on the reel so you can release line when the halibut strikes.

After the strike, the fish feels like a dead weight or snag. Light pressure will sometimes force the halibut to swallow the bait. When you think the fish has the bait down, take the slack out of the line and set the hook, hard! Halibut have bony mouths.

A good tip: If you are fishing on a crowded party boat, *Fish on the downwind side of the boat.* Your line will get to the fish first!

Rock Sole grow to about a pound.

Sole, Sand Dab *[Citharichthys sordidus], and Turbot*
All of the above are flatfish and are found in Southern California waters. Sand dab and sole are taken incidentally while fishing for rock cod in deep water, and on purpose by some determined anglers off Catalina Island. These fish are usually found in 300 feet of water, or more.

Sand dabs grow to about a pound and sole to around 6 pounds. Turbot, small flatfish inhabiting the bays of Southern California, rarely exceed 2 pounds, but all are excellent eating.

Sheepshead: *[Pimelometopan pulchrum]*
A member of the Wrasse family, sheepshead are commonly found around rock and kelp beds. The male is resplendent with a white lower jaw, black head and red and black striped body. The female is usually a uniform pink. These fish have strong, prominent teeth to puncture and crush the shellfish

which provide the main portion of their diet. They achieve a weight of over 30 pounds and are an excellent adversary.

Sheepshead are not considered a good table fish. Their flesh is white and coarse. Many anglers boil them and flake the cold meat for cocktails and salads. They taste a bit like crab this way.

Mussels, squid, shrimp and abalone trimmings make top baits for these fish. They are normally caught in water over 60 feet in depth but may be hooked in the surf and, on occasion, at several hundred feet with rock cod.

Sheepshead are among the fishes that change sexes during their lifetimes, and are one of the few fishes that are easily identifiable as to sex. The smaller fish are almost uniformly pink in color, and are females. The males are very colorful, with black coloration on the head and tail sections, and bright red in the middle of the body, and a white lower jaw. As the females grow, they gradually change color and turn into males. A number of other fish also change sex, such as Giant black seabass and marlin.

Sculpin *[Scorpaena guttata]*
The sculpin is the only venomous fish that is quite common to Southern California waters—venomous may not be technically correct, but comes very close to it. Sculpin are small bottom-dwellers that rarely grow to more than 3 pounds. They're a mottled, rusty-red and white color, and not at all handsome. With large mouth and pectoral fins, and a high, spiny

Sculpin is the only venomous fish that is common to Southern California.

dorsal it practically tells you to "Look out!" The only safe way to handle sculpin is by grasping the lower jaw with the thumb and forefinger. They have no teeth. The spiny fins and rays carry a toxic substance that can cause severe pain, shock and nausea for which there appears to be no remedy except time.

Sculpin are very fine eating and are much sought by fish markets. When the fins are removed and the body skinned, they may be cooked whole. These fish have a very fine, white flesh, but unless you are well experienced with a knife and have seen these fish prepared, *don't try it!* Have the deckhand clean it for you.

Sculpin will take live anchovies but squid is the best bait for them.

Choice locations include rocky reefs and old wrecks in 50 to 75 feet of water. The roe is poisonous.

Cabezon [*Scorpaenichthys marmoratus*]

This fish is a shallow water rock dweller and is common to breakwaters and rocky reefs. Very similar in body conformation to the sculpin, the cabezon has neither poison nor sharp fins.

Cabezon may be red, gray, or lavender in color. Until cooked, the flesh will usually be the color of the skin, turning white in the cooking.

Abalone trimmings, clams and squid are the best bait for these fish. They may be caught by fishing in holes or pockets in the rocks or from breakwaters at low tide. All that is needed is a handline.

Cabezon can reach a weight of about 10 pounds, and are excellent eating. Roe is also poisonous

Ocean Whitefish [*Caulolatilus princeps*]

The ocean whitefish is not related to the whitefish found in fresh water. This is a hardfighting bottom-dweller that is found from Point Conception to Magdalena Bay.

Mark Davis with an unusual albino salmon grouper.

Whitefish attain a weight of about 12 pounds. They are olive to light tan on the back, fading to white on the belly. This fish has a small mouth and head.

Anchovies, pieces of squid or other cut bait are best for whitefish. When they are tough feeders, a fillet of anchovy on a small hook will usually produce the desired results.

Sometimes called "bottom yellowtail" because of their scrappiness, this fish has very sharp, serrated gill covers which can inflict a very nasty cut. *Do not grasp this fish about the head.*
Ocean whitefish are good eating but must be skinned.

Kelp or Calico Bass [*Paralabrax clathratus*]

Kelp or calico bass are common to Pacific Coast waters from Point Conception to mid Lower California. Larger fish will weigh over 10 pounds. They are found over reefs, around rock jetties and breakwaters, as well as in kelp beds. An omnivorous feeder, the kelp bass will take most of the local live baits and a variety of lures. The baits most preferred are squid, anchovy and jack mackerel. They will hit feather jigs (green and yellow), Spoofers (white), Straggler "Choppers" (green and yellow or brown and yellow), clouts, scampi, and other leadhead jigs, and the small "Candy Bar" type lures. Salas' #2X200 in green and yellow is a favorite.

This fish may be caught at any time of day but early morning and late evening are best. The most productive period for fishing around the local breakwaters is from an hour before until about three hours after dark — or later if there is a bright moon! The best times are those days when sundown is closely followed by a bright, full moon.

These breakwater bass, like their offshore cousins, may be taken on a variety of lures and baits. Twin tailed leadhead jigs such as Clouts and Scampis, dressed with a bit of squid, are usually deadly. I also have good success by using just a sliding sinker ahead of a good sized hook, a 3/0 or 4/0, and just the head of a squid, bouncing this combination in and around rocks and kelp. Trolled swimming minnow type lures sometimes produces well, also.

They will take a variety of large baits, including tom cod, herring, Spanish mackerel, smelt, perch, or even small green mackerel. These fish have a large mouth and a 4-pound bass can easily eat a bait weighing as much as a half-pound.

Bass may also be taken by trolling freshwater swimming-type plugs — the yellows and reds seem to be the best colors.

This fish is considered by many to be the best eating fish in local waters. It is a protected species with a size limit of 12 inches. It may be neither bought nor sold.

Recommended tackle for these fish is on the light side. For fishing breakwaters and bays, a light ocean outfit in the 15- or 20-pound line class is more than adequate. Freshwater casting outfits with 12- to 17-pound line also work very well. When fishing from live bait boats, a 7- to 8-foot rod with 15- to 25-pound line is best. You'll want a rod with light tip to cast the bait to the edge of the kelp, and a reel with a plastic or aluminum spool.

Squid, when available, are by far the best bait and are fished in several different ways. When fishing squid you should always use a large hook – 2/0, 3/0, or 4/0 – since small hooks tear out of the bait easily.

I like to use a sliding sinker, rigged right on the line ahead of the hook. Another good method of fishing with squid, either alive or dead, is by employing a clout, another twin tailed leadhead jig. This acts as a sinker to get the bait down and also adds some attraction that seems to work much better than a plain sinker. The relatively new CLOUT lure, with its wide variety of colors, has proven to be a killer for calico and sand bass, as well as other varieties of inshore

Paul Larson, of Huntington Beach, with a 9 lb. Calico Bass taken "on the iron."

fish. The "octopus", "mackeral" and "dolphin" patterns have been particularly effective.

If you are using your own boat to fish for bass, here are a few tips that might help you increase your catch. The larger fish live deep in the kelp beds or back in the rocks. They come out to feed when conditions are right. If you have enough bait for chum you can sometimes lure them from their lair to feed on your offerings. Be sure to position your boat so that your chum (live bait or dead squid) will be carried by the current into the heaviest part of the kelp bed or rock pile you are working – then wait them out. Often it will take the better part of an hour before they start feeding, but you'll find it was worth the wait.

These fish will take full advantage of the kelp when hooked, by wrapping your line around the nearest stalk. If you slack your line and just wait a bit, they will always swim free. This may happen several times but you will, eventually, get the fish.

Barred Sand Bass *[Paralabrax nebulifer]*

Closely related to the kelp or calico bass, sand bass are found in schools on sand flats like those off Huntington Beach and Oceanside. A voracious feeder, they often weigh as much as 8 pounds.

Sand bass will take most baits, but show a definite preference for anchovy or squid. However, this fish will not accept lures as readily as the calico bass. It is often caught against breakwaters.

Almost as good on the table as the calico bass, this fish, too, is a protected species.

Sand bass are taken in fair numbers in bays – such as Newport or Mission Bay – where they are usually caught by casting leadhead jigs with plastic tails, such as clouts.

Spotted Sand Bass *[Paralabrax maculatofasiatus]*

This fish closely resembles the barred sand bass except for small red spots on gill plates, neck, and body. The spotted sand bass rarely exceeds 3 pounds.

Seldom found outside bays, the spotted sand bass is usually caught while casting. It, like the kelp or calico bass and the barred sand bass, is a protected species.

Black Sea Bass *[Stereolepis gigas]*

Black sea bass are the largest of the bass found along the West Coast. They attain a weight of over 500 pounds and are found from the Channel Islands to Baja's Magdalena Bay. They are bottom feeders, will take most bait, but prefer squid, bonito, mackerel, barracuda and whitefish.

Heavy tackle is the rule, as these fish will usually take advantage of rocks and kelp to cut a line. Heavy monofilament is used for the leader because they have no teeth, of note.

Although May through September seems to produce most of the catches in California, these fish are caught year-round in Mexico, both along the coast and at Guadalupe Island. Skin diving reduced the fishery in Southern California until seasonal limits were set on divers.

Black sea bass are relatively slow growing and it's estimated that a 300-pounder is over 20 years old. The adults are a very dark brown, almost black, with bronze overtones; the young (under 50 pounds) are silvery with large purple spots which disappear as the fish dies. They are stubborn but not spectacular fighters, and are excellent eating at any size.

Rocky areas and kelp beds in water from 60 to over 200 feet deep are the popular habitat for these fish. Three of the better areas are: Anacapa Santa Barbara Island and San Nicolas Islands.

Black sea bass are known to feed at night and many fine catches are made after sundown on long-range trips.

In Mexican waters, slab baits of a whole fillet of bonito or yellowtail are particularly effective. These fish are prone to school, and when one is taken, more can be expected.

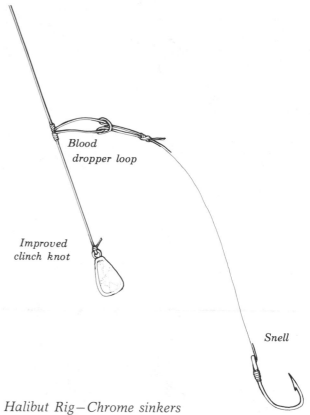

Halibut Rig—Chrome sinkers are usually best

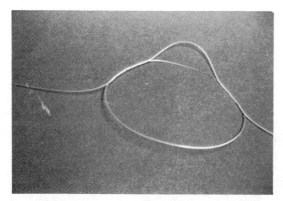 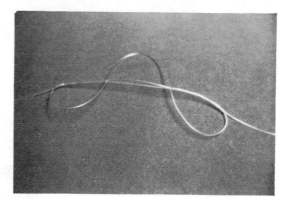

Blood drooper loop, also used to fasten two lines together.

White sea bass make a stubborn, deep fight-usually one or two long runs-and then tire quickly. Jean Hinckley caught these two on the boat "Electra" at Santa Cruz Island

Author and son, Mark, with two Catalina Island white sea bass.

". . .not a spectacualr fighter, they are much sought as a food fish."

Chapter 10
White Sea Bass

White sea bass are closely related to Atlantic weakfish, corvina, and totuava of Mexico, and are common on the West Coast from Point Conception to the Magdalena Bay area of Baja, California. They have been caught off Southern California year-round but the best catches are usually made from January through June.

Early season catches are usually made out of San Diego, near the Coronado Islands. There are also fair numbers of fish taken out of Oceanside and Dana Point. Sometimes these fish are caught in good numbers by boats out of Newport and Long Beach/San Pedro, at the Huntington Beach flats and Catalina Island. From time to time, good runs of white sea bass occur at Rocky Point, the Channel Islands and at Point Conception.

Squid seem to be the key to good white sea bass fishing. The largest catches are made where schools of squid are found, and live squid is by far the best bait.

Night fishing is sometimes the most effective and white sea bass are caught at the same time as the squid that are being used for bait. They are not spectacular fighters, but are sought as a food fish. They make a stubborn, deep fight—usually one or two long runs—and then tire quickly. They will take advantage of kelp, and many fish are lost because of it.

As usual when fishing with squid, large 4/0 or 5/0 hooks should be used. Twenty-five to 40-pound test line is recommended, with a rubber-core or sliding sinker ahead of the hook. White sea bass usually take bait while it is sinking. The customary method is to cast out and let bait sink to the bottom—then retrieve with a stop-and-go motion, using long sweeps of the rod. A three- or four-foot run, before setting the hook, is usually sufficient. Wire leaders are not required.

These fish will occasionally take jigs of the Candy Bar type when worked deeply and slowly. Additional good white sea bass baits when available, are sardines and Pacific green mackerel. A live squid, combined with a clout or other twin tailed leadhead jig, is sometimes very effective.

When picking these fish up, do not put your hand into their extremely sharp gills.

White sea bass grow to over 70 pounds, but a fish of over 50 is unusual.

As squid are frequently mating during the white sea bass season, more than one squid on the hook sometimes works best. Squid are frequently very hard to come by, however, and this practice is frowned upon when bait is scarce. On some occasions I have seen white sea bass taken on gangnions of the same type used for deep water rock cod fishing. Once, at San Diego, I stood next to a fellow who had been out the day before and watched while he caught five nice fish, to 25 pounds, on rock cod gear with 80-pound test dacron line, a big two-pound sinker and five hooks on a gangnion. I was hard pressed to catch one on 20-pound test mono and a smallish (by his standards) 2/0 hook. I finally went to my tackle box in desperation and "haywired" a quick gangnion together by simply making a series of dropper loops and then looping 5/0 hooks on each of the droppers. I put two squid on each hook, as he was doing, and hooked a fish immediately. By that time the bite was over but I had learned a lesson I won't forget.

Mark Davis and Bill Stark with a good catch of Vermillion Rock Fish.

"...rock codding is fun!"

Chapter 11

Rock Fish

Rock Cod [Sebastodes]

The so-called rock cod are not cod at all but members of the rock fish family, which include over 50 different species on the West Coast – most of which are found in California. It would be impossible to describe all of these so we will consider only those of major importance to the Southern California sport fisherman.

In my book – and this is it – rock codding is fun! I have asked myself why and have come to several conclusions: first, the fisherman never knows which kind of fish he is going to catch. Next, there is the possibility – indeed, the likelihood – that a person will catch a large ling cod or huge cow cod. Finally, weather permitting, the rock fish are cooperative critters. You can usually depend on a good catch of fine eating fish at a time of year that does not produce the more sporting surface feeders.

In general, these fish are found in deep water, from about 250 to well over 1,00 feet. They prefer rock pinnacles and reefs but may also be found on the edge of sharp drop-offs, where upwellings bring feed from the surrounding deeper waters.

Rock fish are found with the aid of modern electronic "fish finders" – sonar devices that transmit high frequency sound waves and record the resulting echo from the bottom or from fish in the area. Sonar can locate fish but it cannot make them bite.

Rock cod are usually voracious feeders and a successful catch is frequently just a matter of getting the bait to them. In fairly shallow water this is not too difficult because it does not require a very large sinker to get down 300 feet or less – 12 to 16 ounces of weight is usually sufficient. However, when you are fishing in extreme depths of 600 feet or more, you may find it necessary to resort to several pounds of lead to get down and stay there long enough to "load up" the gangion. One skipper I know recommends one pound for the gangion and one additional pound for each three hooks.

The usual method is to employ a gangion, or long main leader, with a number of short leaders, off of swivels, to make up a long string, with the sinker at the bottom. Some experienced fishermen use as many as 15 hooks. Because these fish have very large mouths, large hooks are the rule. The "Kirby style" hook is the most popular although the long line, or "circle," hooks also work very well.

Bait can be almost anything – strips of mackerel or bonito; fresh dead, salted or live anchovies; squid, alive or frozen; and, perhaps the best of all, fillets of smaller rock fish with the brightly-colored skin left on. Many anglers decorate their hooks with colored balloons (red, white, yellow and blue), plastic worms (blue or white) and plastic skirts of various hues, in addition to bait. Recently, new methods of fishing rockfish have come to my attention, that work very well. Bill Stark, and his crew of anglers from his small store in Tustin, have come up with gangions comprised of leadhead jigs, of about ¼ ounce size, on good sized hooks of perhaps 5/0. These leadheads are dressed with either saran or feathers in bright orange and yellow, and orange or red heads. They call them "jerk jigs". They are fished either as is, or with a bit of squid or other bait. I have found them to be most effective, and in most cases, better than baited hooks. Once dropped to the bottom, the string of jigs is "jerked" up and down, yo-yo fashion, and, I assume, appears to be a small school of shrimp. Whatever, it works for reds, cows and salmon grouper, very well. Shrimp flies, tied to a gangion, also are good producers.

Rock cod do not fight too hard, but, get a good string of 5-pounders and you'll have done some work by the time they pop to the surface.

Once you have located the depth at which fish are feeding, a good trick is to slip a rubber band onto your line as a marker. The fish may be 50 feet or more off the bottom and the rubber band saves you the time and energy it would take to drop all the way down and reel back to where the fish are located. When the fish start biting, give them plenty of time to "load up." The impulse is to start reeling immediately, but remember how far your line is down and have patience. The hooked fish will usually settle down after a few moments of sharp tugs; then, you can feel each new fish as it is hooked. When you think that the line is loaded, you are out of bait or the fish have quit biting, start on up. Slow and steady is the game. Don't pump the fish and don't try to reel too fast or they'll twist themselves off the hooks.

When properly rigged for rock cod you'll have a stout rod of about 7 feet with a roller tip. The reel should be a Penn Senator model of either 6/0 or larger. The number 114H with a long extension handle, for leverage, is a favorite. The reel should be filled to capacity with 60- or 80-pound dacron line. Monofilament stretches so much it is almost impossible to feel the strike or set the hooks, and mono will spread even the toughest of spools when it is wound on under extreme pressure. To complete the outfit, a device called a "railboard" is fastened to the rod just ahead of the foregrip. This is a metal plate, usually plastic-covered to protect the rail, and allows the fisherman to rest the rod on the rail for the long pull upward.

First time "rock codders" should rent an outfit from the landing or boat operator.

If you have your own boat and like to fish for these deep-water fish, the best tackle consists of a rod with roller guides and tip, and wire line. The line can be either Monel single-strand or stranded wire. Seven-strand is manufactured locally. Ninety-pound test wire is ideal, and it's not necessary to use as much lead as with dacron. There is less line drag and, you can feel every nibble—which you can never do with conventional line. Wire is not welcome on the open boats, since it's murder in a tangle.

Now, let's talk about the fish . . .

Vermillion Rock Fish *[Sebastodes miniatus]*

This popular fish, commonly called the "red snapper," is a beautiful brick red, enhanced by large golden eyes. Although it attains a weight of 8 pounds, 5 pounds is average.

The red snapper is valuable commercially as well as with sport fishermen. A very good tablefish, it's usually fried but is highly prized by the Chinese for steaming.

Juvenile fish will be found in shallow water and adults in depths to 600 feet.

Boccacio *[Sebastodes paucispinis]*

Often called "salmon grouper" or "slimies" by deckhands and skippers. They are one of the most abundant of the rock fish species.

The back of the fish is dark brown in color, shading to an orange (or salmon) on sides, and then to a very light orange on the belly. Another very distinguishing feature of the Boccacio is the prominent, under-shot lower jaw. Larger specimens ordinarily have black spots scattered about the body, looking for all the world as though someone had spattered them with tar.

The Boccacio sometimes reaches a weight of over 20 pounds, but a 15-pounder is considered large. These fish are excellent eating but require special care in preparation to make them better than average. They should always be bled immediately after landing so the meat will be pure white when filleted and to prevent a "fishy" odor when cooked. If the bleeding procedure is not followed, the meat has a gray look and a most disagreeable odor while cooking. This fish should always be skinned. *This works for all fish.*

The Boccacio is found from shallow waters to a depth of over 1,000 feet.

Cow Cod

Cow Cod [Sebastes levis]

This, the largest of the rock rish family, attains a weight of over 35 pounds. It is found in very deep water—from 300 to 1,200 feet, usually best at 600 feet.

The fish is a beautiful soft orange with large, golden eyes. About one-third of the cow cod's total weight is head. Its huge mouth and very high prominent dorsal fin make identification easy.

Needless to say, several "cows" on a line are a tough load to handle.

Chili Pepper [Sebastodes goodei]

The chili pepper is another major rock fish. It is found in large schools, and each fish weighs about the same, leading one to believe they must be similar in age.

These fish are found as deep as 1,000 feet. They bite readily and are known to "climb"—that is, to come up with the hooked fish and bite at a shallower depth on each consecutive drop of the bait.

The chili pepper derived its name from the fact that long strings of these bright red fish closely resemble a string of drying chillies. It is a rather slender species when compared to most rock fish and reaches a weight of about 5 pounds. The color is brownish-red on the back, deepening to bright red on the sides, with a narrow pink stripe down the lateral line and white belly.

The fish is, like most of this species, very good eating.

Olive Rock Fish [Sebastes serranoides]

"Johnny bass," one of the most common of the shallow-water rock fish, is a mainstay of the sportfishing fleet from Oxnard north to San Francisco. Johnny bass are caught on the surface, and down to about 500 feet. They are common in midwater, where they hang suspended over reefs and rock piles. They also like kelp beds, in shallow water.

They reach a weight of about 7 pounds and are fine scrappers on light gear. They take lures like Bomber Jigs readily, as well as live anchovies. They strike on the surface near kelp beds, coming out to attack the lure. Many times they will stop the lines of rock codders as they send baits toward the bottom.

This fish is a uniform olive-brown, with faint yellow spots and fins tinged with yellow. An excellent foodfish, it closely resembles the yellowtail rock fish, but is longer and slimmer.

Whitebelly Rock Fish [Sebastis vexilaris]

A chunky member of the rock fish family, the "chucklehead" is a fine fighter and notable on the table. They are taken incidentally, while fishing for rockcod.

They are dull yellow and olive-pink on the back, and are caught in water from 60 to 600 feet deep. They have large mouths and prefer big baits. I have taken many of them on fillets of rock fish while fishing for lingcod, and find them very heavy for their length.

Starry Rock Fish [Sebastes Constellatus]

A rather common deep water fish, the starry rockfish is sometimes known as the "bosco." Small specimens are generally used for bait, after filleting. This fish does not attain any great size, and one of 3 pounds is considered large.

The starry rock fish is bright orange with yellow spots. It has a large head, is easily identified, and makes excellent eating.

Green Striped Rock Fish [Sebastes elongatus]

This is another of the smaller but common species. It is easily identified by its lateral stripes of alternating green and orange and is sometimes called the "poinsettia."

Since this fish rarely weighs as much as 2 pounds it is commonly used as bait, even though good eating.

Flag Rock Fish [Sebastes rubrivinctus]

The flag rock fish, also known as the "barberpole" is one of the prettiest of all deep water fish. It is obviously named for its appearance—vivid vertical markings of red and white. This fish is usually found on rock cod trips and is easily identified.

The similar red banded rock fish [Sebastes babcolli] swims deeper waters—from 900 to almost 1,600 feet—and is not commonly caught on rod and reel.

Attaining a weight of about 3 pounds, the flag rock fish is very good eating. It is a shame it cannot be released, but like all rock fish, it comes to the surface dying or dead. It is found in waters from 100 to 600 feet.

Yelloweye Rock Fish [Sebastes ruberrimus]

Another of the more common species that is liable to show up in the bag is the yelloweye rock fish, known also as the "turkey red" or "goldeneye." This fish is sometimes incorrectly identified as cow cod, because of size and coloration. There are several major differences, however, that make it easy to distinguish between the two species. The color of the yelloweye is brighter, a more red-orange than that of the cow cod. The dorsal fins are not as high and they are not as deeply incised as those of the cow cod. The tail fin is rounded in the yelloweye, the cow cod is convex. Finally, the mouth of the yelloweye is much smaller.

Rock Sole

The yelloweye gets to be about the same size as the cow cod, about 36 inches and well over twenty pounds, but unlike the larger cow cod, large fish are found in fairly shallow water. They inhabit depths of from 150 to 1,200 feet. They are quite common at the Channel Islands and around San Miguel Island. They hit lures well and are also taken on large slabs of cut bait.

A number of other rock fish may show up in the catch including blue rock fish, [*Sebastes mystinus*], widow rock fish [*Sebastes entomalas*], yellowtail rock fish, [*Sebastes flavidus*], and the greenblotched rock fish [*Sebastes rosenblatti*].

These are generally "smallish" fish, weighing up to about 1½ pounds. They are not important to the overall catch, but are good eating and make fine bait.

Along with rock fish you may occasionally catch some of the deep water flatfish. These include the Pacific sandab, [*Citharicthys sordidus*], starry flounder, [*Platichthys stellatus*], rex sole [*Glyptocephalus zachirus*], Rock Sole and several other species of halibut-like fish. These fish, usually caught incidentally while fishing for rock fish, are all excellent eating and some may weigh as much as 20 pounds.

Flat fish do not float like rock fish, and should be gaffed. Do **not** lift out of water.

Additional tips on Rock Cod Fishing:

If the service is available, and it usually is, let the crew fillet your fish on the way in. It will be better table fare and you will be saved the trouble of disposing of the carcasses. Sablefish, common name black cod, are another fish that shows up in the catch. A very oily fish, it is best smoked.

Lately it has been discovered that larger rock cod, like the big cows, will occasionally hit lures better than bait. As a result, it's common to use a heavy lure of chrome or a bright color, letting it sink to the bottom and then yo-yoing it on the bottom. Frequently, jackpot fish are taken in this manner. A bit of fish or squid on the jig will usually increase the jig's effectiveness.

Sharks can be a pest when you are rock codding. The common blue shark will take your fish on the way up and then become entangled in the gangion. When this occurs, see if the crew can save the sinker, then cut loose the rest of the mess. Occasionally bonito sharks will appear, to take fish off the gangion. These speedy predators will usually bite themselves clear. Pinback sharks are a nuisance when the boat drifts off the rocky areas.

Once in a while a deep water octopus is caught on the rock cod grounds. These creatures are an awesome sight but not really dangerous. I have seen them measure as much as 12 feet across and weigh 50 pounds. They are bright orange—the same color as cow cod—and are esteemed by Italian and Portuguese fishermen. I have eaten them pickled in the Japanese manner, and they are delicious. A delicious octopus salad is made by the Slavonian and Italian fishermen of San Pedro.

All in all, while rock codding may not be "sport fishing" in the true sense of the word, no one can deny that it is a sport, and it *is* fishing! Usually done in the winter months when the surface fish are absent or dormant, this activity not only provides healthy outdoor exercise but also fills the freezer with welcome, wholesome fish—some of the best eating there is, in my opinion.

Rock cod are found from Alaska south to mid-Baja, California. They are basically a cold water fish and in

Ling Cod

blue-green mouth and throat. The flesh is the same color as the mouth, until cooked; then it turns snow white.

Ling cod have large teeth which can inflict nasty cuts and puncture wounds. They do not have an air bladder like the rock fish and can ascend from, or descend to, deep water with no ill effects. They are voracious feeders and prefer large baits or lures.

In the northern part of their range, ling cod are found in shallow water but, in Southern California, they are usually taken in deep water along with the rock cod, except at San Miguel Island, near Point Conception.

The Point is a dividing line between the Southern California species and those found only in the north. California lobsters are not found north of here, nor are most of the game fish taken in Southern California.

San Miguel Island provides some of the finest ling cod fishing grounds in the state. Boats from Channel Island Sportfishing, Oxnard, and Sea Landing, Santa Barbara, specialize in fishing ling cod at San Miguel.

Saury—a primary forage fish for albacore, marlin, etc.

their northern ranges are found in comparatively shallow water. South of Point Conception, where the water is normally warm, it is necessary to fish deep for rock cod.

In Southern California they are found at all of the islands, along the edge of the Continental Shelf, as well as the offshore banks extending over 100 miles from shore.

Ling Cod [Ophiodon elongatus]

Still another cod that is not a "cod" is the ling cod, an unusual fish. It is alone in its class and reaches great size, having been reported to weigh up to 70 pounds. An important food fish in the British Columbia and Alaskan fisheries, it is found along the Pacific Coast to Mexico.

The ling cod has a very large mouth and long, sinuous body. Its coloration runs from brown to light blue to dark turquoise, with a mottled appearance much like military camouflage. The skin coloration continues into the interior of the mouth, and it is not unusual to find one of these fish with a bright

Pleagic puffer fish, prime forage fish in tropical waters.

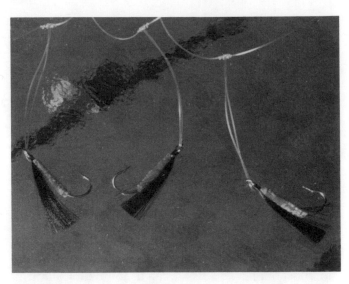

Shrimp fly rig for rock fish

Rock fish "jerk jigs"

and tail intact. Experienced fishermen will use one large bait on a long leader rather than a gangion when fishing specifically for ling cod. Many times a "ling" will seize a small fish that has been hooked and hang on clear to the surface, only letting go at the very top.

Green Spotted Rock Fish

As soon as you see you have a ling cod, call for the gaff. Many times it is possible to capture the fish, even though it is not hooked.

Once, when my two sons and I were fishing for salmon out of Campbell River, British Columbia, we stopped our 14-foot cartopper to see if we could catch a ling for dinner. Using a small portable fish locator, we found a rocky pinnacle about 150 feet down. We dropped 3 aluminum jigs to the bottom and started yo-yoing them up and down. Mark, who was 11 at the time, connected first with a 20-pounder.

We felt very proud of ourselves and went right back to the spot for another drop. This time Steve hooked one. He complained about how hard it was fighting while Mark and I were trying to hook a fish. Steve suddenly yelled that it didn't look like we could get this one into the boat. I looked over the side into a cavernous mouth, and gaffed a 50-pounder.

We gave Mark's fish to some people who were "skunked" and fed half the trailer park with Steve's — besides eating on it ourselves for several days.

A long run, of some 60 miles, the boats must leave early in the morning. It is well worth the ride. In addition to ling cod, island waters abound in rock fish which are caught in relatively shallow water.

Ling cod will hit lures of either chrome or white, along with squid and slabs of cut fish. One of the best baits is a whole fillet of blue rockfish with the skin

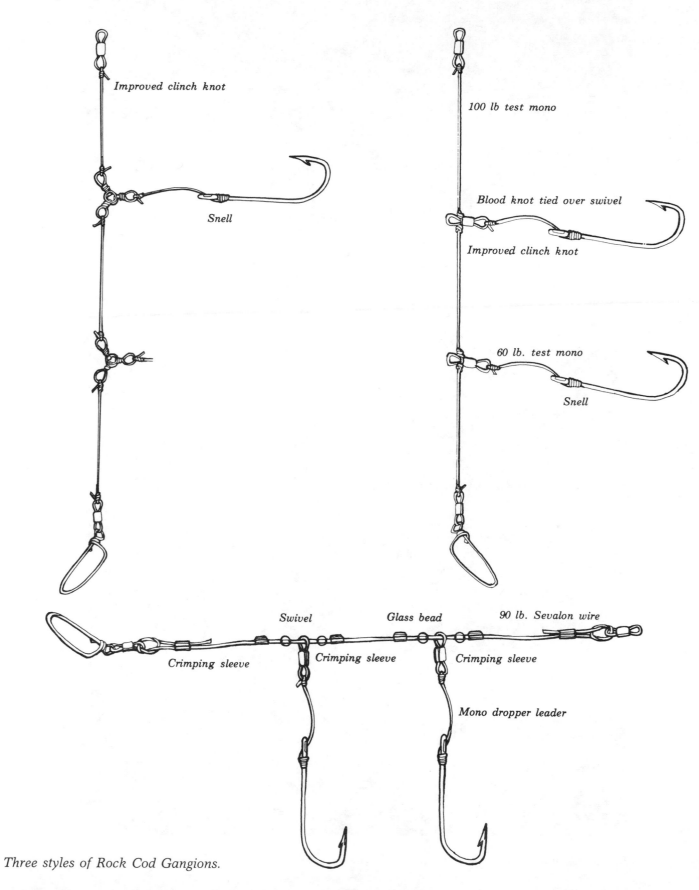

Improved clinch knot

Snell

100 lb test mono

Blood knot tied over swivel

Improved clinch knot

60 lb. test mono

Snell

Swivel *Glass bead* *90 lb. Sevalon wire*

Crimping sleeve *Crimping sleeve* *Crimping sleeve*

Mono dropper leader

Three styles of Rock Cod Gangions.

Bob Ford with a large Clarion Island Wahoo.

"...the wahoo is one of the most exciting fish that swims."

Chapter 12

Wahoo

While the wahoo is not common to Southern California, it is an important fish in the long-range catch, and for that reason is included here. Wahoo range as far north as Alijos Rocks, Baja, but are seldom caught in water of less than 76 degrees. They are common around Cape San Lucas in the late fall and winter months, and year-round at the Rivellagigedos Islands of Mexico.

A memeber of the mackerel family, the wahoo is closely related to the king mackerel of the East Coast as well as Sierra and Spanish mackerel. Like all of these fish, it has savage teeth, and wire leaders are a must. When fishing in wahoo territory, black swivels are mandatory. They will hit anything shiny – slicing it off.

In my opinion, the wahoo is one of the most exciting fish that swims – not the strongest, but one of the fastest and most unpredictable of them all. They hit lures well and will also take live bait.

When fishing the waters mentioned above, the usual method is to troll until fish are located, and then stop and fish for them with cast jigs and live bait in much the same manner as one would seek albacore and tuna. In many instances they will be found mixed with yellowfin tuna.

When trolling, wahoo show a marked preference for lures close to the transom; right in the white water of the prop wash. They like bright, shiny lures and vivid colors. Chromed-head lures such as the large Hex Heads with lively-colored vinyl skirts work very well. Equally desirable are the scoop-nosed plugs that are favorites with Hawaiian anglers.

After several trips into Wahoo country I have found that bright red, and red and yellow combinations seem to work the best – although, at times, they will hit anything. For casting lures, chrome is by far the best. We also found that adding prismatic tape to the lures increases their effectiveness. I have decided that a large, single hook is better than the trebles that come on the lures. Wahoo have a tough mouth and are notorious for throwing the jig. The small bite of the treble doesn't seem to hold. I use an 8/0 or 9/0 openeye salmon hook, Mustad No. 9510XXX. Be sure to use wire ahead of all lures – 10 to 12 inches is about right.

I have said that wahoo are unpredictable, and here are a few examples. When trolling, many times a fish will come out of the water as high as 10 or 12 feet to land on a jig. Sometimes there will be three or four fish in the air at one time. On occasion a wahoo will attack a lure from below and leap higher than your head when striking. I've had fish take the lure right against the boat, and on a number of occasions, they've leaped into our craft by following the lure as it was lifted aboard. I saw one fish, weighing about 40 pounds, make at least a 30-foot jump and clear a rail 10 feet above the water in pursuit of a jig being retrieved by Paul Morris of San Diego. Paul now has that fish on his wall. Needless to say, we were all very careful when lifting jigs out of the water for the rest of the trip.

When hooked, the wahoo is equally spectacular. Fished with reasonable tackle, say 40-pound test line and a Jigmaster reel with matching rod, a 40- to 60-pound wahoo is a real heart-stopper. It will fight right on the surface of the water and is capable of terrific speed. It is not uncommon to see an angler in futile pursuit of a wildly running wahoo as it outraces the panting fisherman around the boat. You just cannot outrun a wahoo. The line makes a rooster tail as the spool melts of line. After a couple of these runs, the fish will slow down and can be pumped to the boat – if you have managed to stay with it.

The wahoo is one of the best eating of all fish caught on long-range trips. They are delicious barbecued or smoked, and may be frozen or canned upon return to port. If you are planning to fish in wahoo country, be sure to take lots of tackle. The teeth and savage strikes of these fish destroy lures at a terrific rate. A double handful of extra skirts will allow you to repair lures in the evening.

The author caught this dolphin from the boat "Tick-Tock" south of San Diego.

". . .noted for beauty, fighting ability and superb table quality."

Chapter 13
Dolphin

Dolphin are caught only occasionally in Southern California waters, and only in years abnormally high water temperatures. Those years that produce yellowfin tuna will usually supply dolphin. Most of the long-range trips that go below Point Eugenia in Baja (see map) find dolphin, the fish known as "mahi-mahi" in Hawaii and as "dorado" in Mexico.

The dolphin is noted for its beauty and fighting ability as well as superb eating qualities. Dolphin attain a size of over 60 pounds, but a 40-pounder is considered large.

These fish hit lures quite well and prefer one that creates some surface commotion, like the Kona Head and Knucklehead types. Red and yellows, and green and yellow combinations provoke the most strikes.

Dolphin have a peculiarity that helps to produce fish on many a day that would otherwise be fruitless — the propensity to lie under flotsam on the surface. Even a small piece of driftwood or paper carton will often produce a fish or two. I once rented a small outboard boat, with native skipper, near San Jose Del Cabo in Baja, California (see map) and we caught fish after fish by trolling lures past the buoys of local shark fishermen and these buoys were no more than 12 inches in diameter.

Kelp "paddies" (large patches of floating kelp which have broken loose from the bottom) will usually have dolphin under them in the years these fish invade our local waters. Another nice thing about dolphin is the way they will hang around a boat they have located which has a hooked fish or live bait chum.

From your own boat, a lure presented to dolphin following a hooked fish will almost always draw a strike, presenting a splendid opportunity to catch these fish with either very light tackle or a fly. I have taken several on flies in this manner.

Dolphin put up a strong and determined fight if caught on reasonable gear. Unfortunately, they are too often caught incidently while trolling with heavy gear for other offshore fish. A 25- or 30-pound Dolphin on 12- or 20-pound line will come fairly close to the boat, once, and then will put up a good running and jumping fight.

When you catch your first dolphin, take the time to really inspect the fish. In water the colors are predominantly blue and green with neon blue edges on the fins. Once in the boat, however, wave after wave of indescribable color washes over the sides of the fish until it dies. It is a never-to-be forgotten sight.

Dolphin make a beautiful wall mount.

A jumpin marlin, on the end of a line, is not soon forgotten. [Photo by Dr. Bob McCoy]

"Early in this century, the first marlin were caught around Catalina Island."

Chapter 14
Marlin

The striped marlin is another fish that is under a great deal of pressure, worldwide.

Although not considered a prime eating fish in this country, the marlin is highly regarded as a food fish in Japan where it is used in a sausage similar to our weiners.

"Longliners" annually take thousands of tons of these fish and, as a result, the size of the fish has been diminished. However, there is still a good fishery in Baja and occasionally in Southern California.

Early in this century the first marlin were caught around Catalina Island — the home of big game sportfishing. These first fish were caught with very primitive tackle and trolled flying fish for bait. Some were caught from rowed skiffs! With the advent of the outrigger, in the thirties, this became the accepted method: troll dead flying fish from the outriggers, and drop the bait back to the fish before setting the hooks.

When fishing was resumed after World War II, live bait was introduced and many fish were caught by casting live sardines or mackerel to feeding fish — but the trolled flying fish was still the most popular method.

Over the past few years most marlin caught in Southern California waters have been taken on lures trolled at relatively high speeds. There are a number of very fine marlin lures available, including "Clones," "Konehead," "Psychedelic," etc.

Marlin show up in Southern California waters in early July and may stay as late as December, depending upon water temperatures and food. They are available in Baja year-round, apparently migrating from mid-Pacific waters. Extensive tagging has been done and most tag returns are from the 800-boat Japanese long-line fleet which ranges the entire Pacific Ocean. It is significant that no fish tagged in Mexican waters have been recovered in Southern California, while Southern California-tagged fish have been recovered in Mexico. Apparently this proves that marlin migrate in to our coast and then continue on to Mexico.

When marlin are around, they are usually seen. They do a lot of free jumping and evidently spend most of the time close to the surface. They are frequently seen "sleeping" with the tail and hump of the shoulders out of the water as well as "tailing downswell," — almost body-surfing in a good-sized swell. Sleepers can be caught by sliding up to them very slowly, no wake, and casting a live bait. If the fish sees the bait rather than the boat your chances for a strike are excellent. Sardines and Spanish or green mackerel work well in this maneuver. On one occasion, Ralph Clock took two fish from the same school of sleepers by keeping an eye on the school while fighting the first fish. The school stayed up long enough to land the first fish, and then another member of the school readily took a bait.

At times they will "school up" to feed on bait fish such as anchovies, sardines or mackerel and will cause a great commotion on the surface — drawing birds, seals and fishermen. These "feeders" can drive you crazy. If marlin are feeding on anchovies, many times they will not take the larger baits. At other times schools of feeders will pop up and then disappear so quickly that it is impossible to get baits to them. In this situation you can either run from one bunch to

Paul and Cheryl Albrecht with a mornings catch of marlin taken off of Catalina Island.

the next, hoping to get to a feeding fish in time, or slowly troll live mackerel in the general area. Perhaps the best method is to use high-speed trolling lures and cover as much ground as possible.

When using lures for marlin an entirely different technique is employed than with bait. Lures may be trolled straight back or from outriggers, and line as light as 20-pound test may be used successfully. However, 30- to 50-pound test is recommended to set the hook. When trolling lures, set reel drag at approximately one-third of the breaking strength of the line measured *Off the tip of the rod.* When a fish strikes, instead of slowing the boat down or stopping, increase speed immediately and run out 200 to 300 yards of line against the drag. This action will keep constant pressure on the fish even though it is jumping and generally raising hell. Since the marlin has a very hard jaw, and a lot of fish are hooked either in the bill or on the outside of the mouth, it is necessary to apply this pressure to set the hook well.

Sharp hooks are another must. Most manufacturers of marlin lures go to great pains to sharpen the hooks to a needle point. A noted West Coast light tackle big

A mixed Southern California catch of Big Eye Tuna, Marlin and Yellowfin Tuna.

game angler, Al Tetzlaff, sharpens his hook points with a belt sander down to the shape of a regular sewing needle for use with 6- and 12-pound test line for trolling. He has successfully landed many marlin and "sails" with these hooks.

Once the fish is well hooked, the boat is brought around in a gradual turn to pursue the fish and allow the angler to start regaining line.

With my two sons in our own boat at Rancho Buena Vista, Baja, California, we caught marlin every day for four days and, once hooked, did not lose a single fish. All were on 40-pound test line.

It is a good idea to carry tagging equipment when marlin fishing. Tags are available from:

National Marine Fisheries Service
South West Fisheries Center
P.O. Box 271
La Jolla, California 92037

"The slide" off of the East end of Catalina Island is one of the most famous marlin grounds in the world.

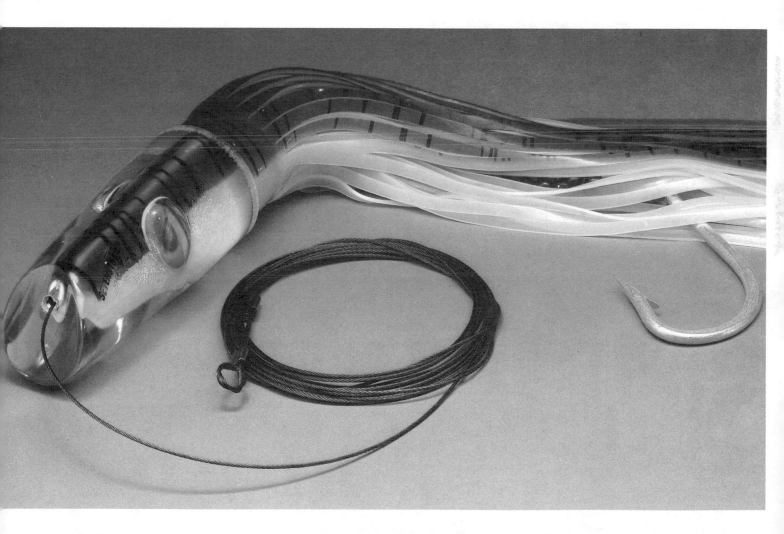

Over the past few years most marlin caught in Southern California waters have been taken on lures trolled at relatively high speeds. This is a "Kona Clone" by Sevenstrand Tackle Corp.

Finning broadbill swordfish. [Photo by Al Tetzlaff]

Fining marlin. [Photo by Al Tetzlaff]

"...the number one big game trophy."

Chapter 15
Swordfish

Although this is really not intended as a "big game" fishing book, the broadbill swordfish, is included because it is found in local waters. Of worldwide distribution in temperate and tropic seas, the broadbill rates as the number one big game trophy with most anglers. Relatively few of the fish are caught each year by sport fishermen, but a great many are taken by harpoon and longline for commercial markets, and recently by gill nets.

The broadbill does most of its feeding in deep, offshore waters where it dines on squid, hake and other deep water fish. When seen on the surface the broadbill is apparently not in a feeding mood, as it only rarely takes a bait. The bait must be presented in such a manner as not to "spook" the fish, and any undue disturbance such as bait splashing on the surface or the boat's wake rolling over the fish will usually sound it.

Bonito, large squid, barracuda and small tuna or albacore make the best broadbill baits.

These fish are distinguished by their prominent dorsal fin and upper tail lobe. Once seen, a broadbill cannot be mistaken for any other fish — and they're the toughest thing that swims. My father battled one for 13 hours and five minutes — only to lose it. Some fights lasting over 24 hours have been recorded. Swordfish caught in California waters rarely weigh over 500 pounds, although the current world record stands at 1,182 pounds with a fish taken by Lou Marron at Iquique, Chile, in 1953.

Broadbill rarely give up at the end of a line. They are not only determined fighters but are also unpredic-table. Most fish display certain characteristics in a fight, but the broadbill will battle in a variety of ways. Although not known as a jumper, swordfish frequently free-jump. This is not the graceful, bounding leap of the marlin or sailfish, but a ponderous heaving of the body out of the sea. Swordfish usually jump straight up and fall back on their side, raising a mighty spout of water. A hooked broadbill will sometimes jump repeatedly — an awesome sight.

The toughest of these fish to land are those that merely swim on the surface and allow you only so close to them. They will sometimes come up under the boat and rub themselves on the keel.

My one bit of advise: when hooked to a broadbill you will get one chance at the boat with the gaff, and sometimes fairly easily. Take it! Even if you feel that the fish is green and not ready for the gaff — gaff him anyway. You have to hurt them, to kill them. They just won't give up.

Nothing under 80-pound test tackle is recommended for this extremely powerful species, and because of their soft mouths, large hooks are standard.

During the past two years, with the reappearance of the Pacific mackerel as a baitfish, many broadbill have been hooked with these live baits. It now appears that a live "green" mackerel is the best possible bait for Southern California broadbill.

A fact all successful commercial swordfishermen soon learn is useful to sport anglers. Broadbill will not fin in southeast winds strong enough to throw whitecaps.

The growing sport of fishing the ocean with a flyrod is both challenging and rewarding. Here Nick Curcione fights a shark on light gear.

". . .the thresher shark is a fine game fish and is excellent eating."

Chapter 16
Shark

Blue Shark *[Prionance glauca]*
This most common of all sharks found in Southern California waters is seen with fins out, on the surface, at any time of year, usually in water over 100 feet deep. They range in size from the newly-born specimen of about one foot, up to 13 feet, and to weights in the hundreds of pounds. They are a nuisance when fishing for rock cod in the winter months and for albacore in the summer, as they will take fish from your hooks. They are not good food fish. *Although if bled when caught they're edible.*

Blue shark are, as the name suggests, a light blue in color on back and sides, shading to a white underbelly. A longish, rounded nose and large pectoral fins make this shark easy to identify. They are sluggish fighters, but put up a reasonable scrap on light gear.

Blue sharks bear their young alive, as do most sharks of the open ocean, and it is not uncommon to have a deck full of the little varmints after landing a large specimen. A word of caution: even the newborn have dangerous teeth and extreme care should be employed when handling any shark. A good practice is to shoot them, or sever the spinal column with a knife before bringing aboard. Sharks are a lower form of life and it is never safe to assume that a shark is dead. Wire leaders are a must for all shark fishing.

Bonito Shark *[Isurus oxyrinchus]*
Of worldwide distribution in temperate seas, the bonito shark rates with many anglers as a game fish. They are wary, jump repeatedly and are fine eating. The bonito shark is closely related to the highly esteemed mako shark of the eastern seaboard and Australia. They are usually found in blue water, with schools of albacore or tunas and on the marlin grounds.

They are a steely blue on the back with a sharp nose and long, pointed teeth; not triangular, as in many sharks. The body conformation is short and powerful with a keel on each side of the tail. Bonito shark range in size to over 1,000 pounds but are rarely seen in excess of 200 pounds in local waters. They will hit a trolled bait or lure and may also be taken drift fishing.

They, too, can be pests while albacore or rock cod fishing. They bite off the tail of a hooked albacore and then tear chunks out of the fish before you can get it aboard. They don't often come close to the surface, and are difficult to shoot or gaff.

The only thing to do is get a wire leader and catch them — having a lot of fun while doing it.

Leopard Shark *[Triakis semifasciata]*
This is a fine shark that is commonly taken in the surf or in shallow water outside beach areas near offshore islands. It is common in Mexico, and as far north as Oregon. It reaches a length of about 6¼ feet and a weight of over 75 pounds. It is rather slender and its brownish-gray body with irregular dark spots make this an easy fish to identify.

They are fairly good fighters, fine eating, and will take squid and mackerel.

Thresher Shark *[Alopias vulpinus]*
Another shark that is a fine game fish, the thresher, has an extremely long upper lobe of the tail — usually as long as the body of the fish, and is found both in open water and inshore.

They are caught at the mouth of the Los Angeles River, in Long Beach Harbor and in Santa Monica

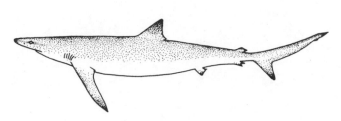

Blue Shark

Bay. In the late fall and winter there are concentrations of these fish at Goleta, and below Oxnard. When there are threshers in the area, they may be seen jumping and occasionally slashing small bait fish with their long, whiplike tail.

Slow-trolling a mackerel, or drift fishing, produce best results. A long leader is a must, because of the tail. These fish are quite selective about taking bait, have a small mouth, and can't handle a hook that is too large. They are fine fighters and often jump repeatedly when hooked.

The thresher is excellent eating and commercial fishermen receive a good price for them.

Thresher sharks are listed with the IGFA, and the current world record stands at 729 pounds. Fish of over 900 pounds have been recorded. The largest I know of in California was just under 400 pounds. When I was fishing commercially, for swordfish, years ago, I harpooned a shark that dressed out over 350 pounds. In the late forties I saw an exceptionally large thresher shark in front of the power plant at the east end of Catalina Island one night when I was fishing for mackerel. Although I had live mackerel for bait, this huge fish refused it. I estimated it to be in the 500-pound class, but things can be deceptive at night.

Recently, a few fishermen have been successful by using downriggers and trolling for threshers.

Smooth Hammerhead Shark [Sphyrna zygaena]

The hammerhead has just recently been recognized as a game fish by the IGFA. They're common to most temperate seas and are common along the Southern California coast and into Mexican waters as far as the Cape San Lucas area and on into the Gulf. I have seen Mexican shark fishermen take them in near Rancho Buena Vista.

Hammerheads arrive in late summer and stay on into fall. They are easily identified by the grotesque hammer-shaped heads with the eyes on the ends of the hammer and wide, tooth-filled mouths underneath. Hammerheads have a prominent triangular dorsal fin that is sometimes taken for swordfish by the unitiated. The tail rarely shows when a hammerhead fins.

These are swift, open-ocean predators and fine

fighters. The broad planing surface of the head makes it tough to land them. They grow to great size, having been reported over 11 feet in length. I have seen these sharks in our local waters that I would estimate in the 500- to 600-pound range. I have taken hammerhead sharks weighing over 200 pounds on rod and reel—and they are tough. Slowly troll a bait into their path, as you would for swordfish, and then stop, allowing the bait to settle. They are sometimes quite wary and will not always take. A small bonito or mackerel makes good bait.

This shark, like most open-ocean species, is dangerous and should be handled with great care at the boat. Large hammerhead jaws are a sought-after trophy.

They are reputed to be good eating, the markets in California are just starting to deal in them.

Sharks in General

There are many more sharks that inhabit waters off the California coast—large and small—but the ones mentioned above are the most common.

Great white sharks, "the maneater," have been taken from local waters and there have been authenticated attacks by sharks off San Francisco and at Guadalupe Island that were traceable to the "white death" as he is known—but they are nowhere plentiful.

If you fish long-range trips into Mexico, you will doubtless come in contact with more of these vicious ocean predators. The rule of thumb is that the farther down into the warm water, the more and bigger the sharks. At the Revillgigedos, sharks have actually driven us out of certain areas, making it impossible to

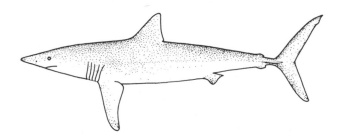

Bonito Shark

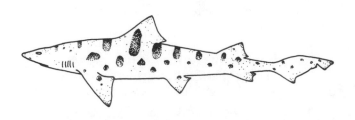

Leopard Shark

Bank Rock Fish—also called "Widow Rock Fish"

Green Spotted Rock Fish

Starry Rock Fish

Sheepshead

Yelloweye Rock Fish—"Turkey Red" or "Goldeye"

Olive Rock Fish—"Johnny Bass"

Chili Pepper—Long strings of these resemble drying chilies

Cow Cod—the largest of the rock fish family

White sea bass are closely related to Atlantic weakfish, corvina, and totuava of Mexico, and are common along the West Coast from Point Conception to the Magdalena Bay area of Baja California. Pat Nash caught this one in Kino Bay, Sonora Mexico. [Photo by Neff Nash]

The vermillion rock fish, commonly called the "red snapper", is a beautiful brick red, enhanced by a large golden eye. This fish was caught near Santa Rosa Island from the boat "Ranger 85".

When you catch your fish dolphin, take the time to really inspect the fish. In water the colors are predominately blue and green with neon blue edges on the fins. Once on the boat, however, wave after wave of indescribable color wash over the side of the fish. The author's son Steve caught this dolphin from the Boat "Tick-Tock" near San Diego.

The bonito shark are closely retlated to the mako shark and are fine eating. The author's son Mark caught this shark while aboard the sportfisher "Searcher" while trolling for albacore.

Nick Curcione of Hermosa Beach has discovered that corbina, along with surf perch, will take an orange fly. He fishes from the breaker line to the foam at his feet, and believes most surf fishermen fish too far out. [Photo courtesy of Nick Curcione]

Surf perch are both popular and prevalent along the beaches of Southern California. These barred surf perch were caught near Hermosa Beach. [Photo by Nick Curcione]

For those anglers who want the thrill of big fish but wish to stay in calm water, bays provide some fine fishing. Channel Island Sportfishing Landing [CISCO], is one of the locations providing access to good fishing.

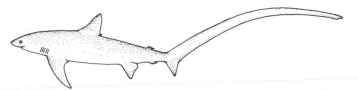

Thresher Shark

land a fish. Some sharks will actually follow the boat and wait for a game fish to hit trolled lures. We have even taken white tip and bull sharks while trolling at over seven knots!

On one such trip a good friend, Nick Ellowitt, hooked a large yellowfin tuna on a trolled lure and before we could stop the boat, sharks had destroyed the tuna right on the surface where we could see the entire drama—leaving only a bloody spot in the water. All that you can do in such a case is pull in all lines and run for a new area.

Sharks will feed any time of day or night, but they become especially active after the sun goes down.

I have found that any fish which breaks the surface in shark-infested waters becomes an immediate target. In the case of wahoo and tuna, I can avoid

sharks by immediately throwing the reel out of gear and allowing the fish to run as hard as possible—usually outdistancing the killers.

Off the Southern California coast, sharks may be chummed with ground fish or squid, and a mixed bag may be expected. These chummed sharks will take large white flies, and are great sport on a fly rod. Any shark to be kept for eating should be bled and cleaned immediately.

Mark Davis with a good size Hammerhead Shark

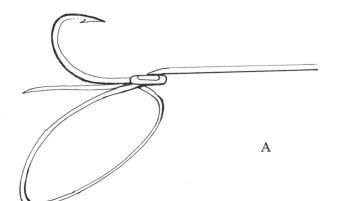

A

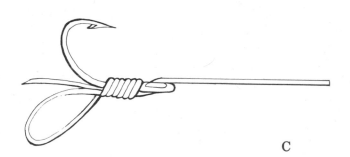

C

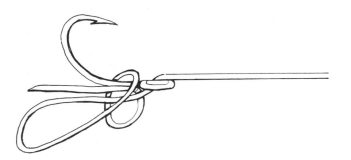

B

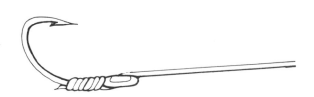

D

The "Snell" knot

Opaleye are easily identified by their olive-green coloration, a bright blue eye and one or two white spots on the back near the dorsal fin. Mark Davis with a nice one caught at the Long Beach Breakwater.

"...for those who prefer solid ground under their feet."

Chapter 17
Surf Fishing

Southern California surf fish provide fine angling for those who prefer solid ground under their feet. There are a number of species available to the surf caster and most of them are excellent on the table.

Kelp bass *[Paralabrax clathratus]:* Although not considered a true surf fish, the kelp or calico bass is rapidly coming into prominence with many surf anglers. It is now known that large bass inhabit very shallow water around rocky areas, and knowledgeable fishermen are pursuing them with a variety of lures. Lead heads with plastic tails work well, and so do a number of aluminum jigs such as Salas, Straggler and Tady. Jigs that have a lot of rolling and darting action with a slow retreive seem to produce the best, in color combinations of green and yellow and blue and white. Some of the preferred spots are the entire Palos Verdes Peninsula, Dana Point and the rocky shoreline at Laguna Beach.

The California corbina *[Menticirrhus Undulatus]* is one of the best. Ranging in weight to 7 pounds, corbina feed on sand crabs and other small baits stirred up by breakers as they crash into the shore, and are most successfully fished right in the white water. Softshell sand crabs, avaialble at shoreside bait stores, are the best bait. Corbina will also take bloodworms, mussels and crabs. Nick Corcione of Hermosa Beach has discovered that corbina, along with surf perch, will take an orange fly. He fishes from the breaker line to the foam at his feet, and believes most surf fishermen fish too far out. Some light tackle enthusiasts fish very light line with mussels and no sinker.

Croaker: The largest of these surf fish is the spotfin croaker, *[Rocador Stearnsii]* reaching about 10 pounds in weight. It is a fine sport and food fish, but is not easy to catch. It feeds largely at night with the incoming tides. Good baits for this fish are razor clams, mussels and ghost shrimp. The croaker next in importance is the **yellowfin** *[Umbrina Rocador]* — a small fish which weighs up to 3 pounds. The yellowfin is also a surf feeder but is a little less selective than spotfin. Yellowfin will take pieces of anchovy, fresh or salted.

A third member of the family, the **black croaker,** *[Cheilotrema Saturnum]* occasionally is taken, but only incidentally. Black croaker do not get much above 2 pounds in weight.

Surf perch are both popular and prevalent along the beaches of Southern California. There are large numbers of these fish that are notable because they bear their young alive. These small young come out into the hostile world of the breakers fully formed and capable of taking care of themselves. The most popular perch in our waters is the **barred surf perch,** *[amphistichus Orgenteus].* This fish may attain a weight to 4½ pounds and is highly prized as a food fish, particularly by Japanese who use it as sashimi. The **calico surf perch,** *[Amphistichus Koelzi]* and numerous others are common to most beaches and rocky areas. Surf perch will take a wide variety of baits. Mussels, sand crabs, bloodworms, clams and ghost shrimp are all good baits. Perhaps one of the best is sugar-cured mackerel, which you will have to prepare for yourself, as it is unavailable in bait stores.

Around rocky surf areas, as opposed to beaches, there are a number of other perch such as the **rubberlip surf perch, rainbow surf perch, pile perch** and others, that readily take mussels, small crabs and worms. All of these fish are fine eating but should be skinned prior to cooking.

Methods for fishing vary but slightly. Baitholder-type hooks from size 6 up to 2/0, depending on the bait, are best. Two dropper leaders off the main line, with the sinker below, comprise the basic surf rig. (See illustration). Sinkers vary with the type of bottom: The surf lug or bulldozer type for open surf, and spoon or flat sinkers in rocky areas. When fishing in extremely rocky places, spark plugs make inexpensive weights, and when tied on with light line, allow hooks and fish to be saved.

Yellowfin Croaker

Barred surf perch [top] and corbina [bottom] caught on flies in the surf [Photo Nick Curcione]

Assortment of surf bait, clockwise from knife—bloodworms, co-host shrimp, salted anchovy, razor clams, butter clam and bay mussels.

In some areas the **opaleye** is also available. This fish is usually called a perch, but really is not. It belongs to a different family, known as the "nibblers." Opaleye are hard fighters and very pugnacious. They live and feed right in the white waters of the most rocky areas, feeding on worms, shirmp and crabs dislodged by wave action. This is where to place your bait. Opaleye are rather omnivorous in that they also feed on moss, which often makes the best bait. Curiously enough, they will also take frozen green peas, sometimes to the exclusion of other baits. Mussels are also a producer.

Opaleye are easily identified by their olive-green coloration, a bright blue eye and one or two white spots on the back near the dorsal fin. This explains the local name, "button perch." Around anchorages such as Avalon on Catalina Island, they are not used for the table because of their habit of feeding on the waste from achored yachts.

The tides influence feeding times of most surf fish. Best fishing is usually on the incoming tide when fresh food is stirred up by the surf.

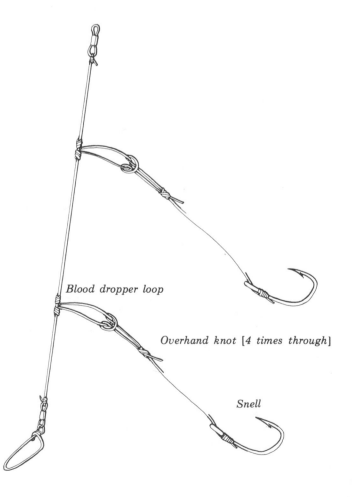

Blood dropper loop

Overhand knot [4 times through]

Snell

Typical surf rig

Nick Curcione holding a corbina he caught on a fly near Hermosa Beach.

Left Angelo Cuanang, right Ski Ratto with a limit of San Fransico stripers. Photo Abe Cuanang.

Chapter 18
Striped Bass

Sriped bass [*Roccus saxatilis*] or "stripers" as they are called, are not native to the Pacific Ocean, but were introduced from the Atlantic Seaboard to the waters of San Francisco Bay with two small plantings, totaling less than 1,000 young fish, in 1879 and 1882. A great fishery developed in the bay area as a result of these plantings, and they spread north to Coos Bay, Oregon, as well. Stripers are anadromous fish, meaning that they need freshwater to spawn. Young fish spend their early lives in the rivers and estuaries of their birth, and then migrate to the sea. They can, and sometimes do live in freshwater all of their lives, and reproduce, but they cannot reproduce in salt water. Some populations of stripers are found in most states with any warmwater fisheries having been introduced, sometimes by accident, into many major river systems. The California Department of Fish and Game is currently planting young stripers in various ocean areas of Southern California, in the hopes that they will provide angling for inshore and bay fishermen. Since they cannot reproduce in the Southern California marine environment, constant plantings will be necessary to provide a consistent fishery. The fish being planted are of about 7 inches in length, and they should grow to approximately 8 or 10 pounds after three or four years in the ocean. Stripers are omniverous and opportunistic feeders, with large mouths and appetites. They will take almost any small fish, alive or dead. They strike artificial lures well, and are one of the relatively few saltwater fish that readily strike surface plugs, which sometimes makes for very exciting fishing. They are considered by many to be among the best eating of saltwater fishes, and are highly prized by gourmets.

The current world record is for a fish of 78 pounds, from the East Coast, and the California record is a fine fish of 65 pounds, taken in 1951 from the San Juaquin River, by Wendell Olsen, of Turlock. In visiting with John Sunada, State fisheries biologist who is working on the Striped bass project, I learned that Stripers are being planted in a number of locations, including King Harbor, at Redondo, Alamitos Bay in Long Beach and at several locations in the San Diego area. Stripers appear to be fish that don't migrate to any great degree, according to Sunada, and remain in close proximity to the areas in which they are planted. Some earlier plantings have produced some good returns of fish from Newport's back bay and the mouth of the San Diego River. Young stripers are raised to planting size in the Elk Grove Hatchery, near Sacramento, and then transported to the planting site via tank truck. They are gradually indoctrinated to saltwater during the trip. I was fortunate to observe a planting of 5,000 of these juvenile fish on January 26, 1982, in King Harbor. The planting was in the dark, at 8:00 P.M., and the fingerlings, some wearing bright yellow tags, seemed to adapt very well to their new environment, and were to be seen under the lights of the docks, swimming actively. If this program succeeds, Southern California anglers may soon experience the thrills of catching large fish from the surf, as do the anglers of the East Coast and Northern California; a whole new breed of fishermen may well develop. In Northern California, it is quite common during the summer months for large schools of stripers to drive schools of baitfish into the surf, and thus create fine angling for surfcasters. Stripers are strong and determined fighters, and are not lead to net or beach easily. They will be most welcome in Southern California.

Pismo clams are fine eating and make delicious chowder. They may be as much as 6 inches across and weigh well over a pound.

"Grunion are a local phenomenon that many people do not believe exist."

Chapter 19

Odds N Ends

With a coastline as long and varied as the one we have endeavored to cover, there are many more fish than it is possible to discuss. We have tried to cover the most important species to the sportfisherman, but there are a few loose ends left.

Grunion are a local phenomenon that many people do not believe exist. The grunion *[Leuresthes tenuis]* is a small smelt-like fish that has the strange habit of spawning on comparatively dry land. They come in on certain moon-drenched (romantic) nights, at the height of the highest tide of the month, and on the largest breakers of that highest tide. At the beginning of a "set" of big waves (which usually come in threes and sevens) female grunion swim to the shore edge of the breaker. Then, as the wave recedes, she digs her body, tail first, down into the moist sand and waits for the next wave, and a mate. With the second wave the males swarm ashore like a navy landing party in search of the girls. As this second wave recedes, the male finds and curls around the female and the two deposit sperm and roe into the sand. Then, on the next wave they both return to mother ocean. Fertilized eggs remain in the warm, moist sand above high tide for about a month until the next high tide when the embryo fish are released from the sand to start the cycle anew.

Grunion may be gathered only by hand—no nets or trapping devices may be used—and a fishing license is required. Since grunion don't always come in to the same beaches, and bright lights are said to deter them, many people think that grunion hunting is akin to a "snipe hunt." Not so. They are fine eating when fried crisp.

For the gatherer there are clams and abalone, but with the huge population of the Southern California area, they have been pretty badly picked over. There is some good clamming available south of the famous Pismo Beach—in fact, within sight of some of the most heavily populated areas of the coast. I'm not going to give away the location of these spots but I will tell you to get a tide book, and if you are really interested, drive up and down the beaches and look for clammers at minus tides. Take a pair of binoculars and I'm sure you will find us digging away with clamming forks. There is a size and possession limit so check the regulations before you start digging. This activity, too, takes a license.

Pismo clams are fine eating and make delicious chowder. They may be as much as 6 inches across and weigh well over a pound. There are other smaller clams and cockels in bays, sloughs, and estuaries— all fine eating. *Be sure to check regulations.*

Lobster, too, were once abundant along our coast and there are still quite a few for the adventurous. Sportfishermen may take them by hand or hook and line, but only during the winter season. Skindivers do best, but if that is not your inclination, they may be taken (if you know how) with hook and line. Lobsters are nocturnal feeders and will rarely be found in the open during daylight hours. Right at sundown, however, they come out to feed on whatever died and sank to the bottom during the day.

Abalone is the best bait for lobster. If ablone is not available, any oily fish will do, such as bonito. The rig consists of a large, *sharp,* treble hook on the bottom and a smaller treble hook about 10 inches up from

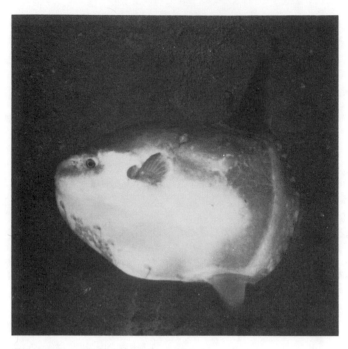

The ocean sunfish, mola mola.

the first one. The bait is securely fastened to the upper treble only. The whole rig is dropped to the bottom, then raised so that the lower hook is on the bottom

but the upper hook is not. The lobster comes to feed on the suspended bait and is right over the large lower hook. With a stout rod and strong line it is possible to drive the lower treble into the soft underside of the tail of the lobster. Result: lobster for dinner!

Lobsters are commonly found around piers, rock jetties, moorings and any kelp bed.

Giant kelpfish and striped kelpfish look like a frond of kelp and are worth a good look. The kelp fish are truly beautiful and a master's work of disguise. They blend perfectly with the habitat, and are good eating, if skinned, but so pretty that I usually release them.

These two fish are common in Southern California and upper Baja waters wherever there are large stands of kelp. The giant kelpfish is the most common on live bait boats and grows to 24 inches in length.

Sometimes, when fishing inshore at the islands, with cut bait, you will be bothered by small orange fish that school up about your hook and strip it clean. These are senorita *[Osyjulis californica].* They are pretty little pests and quite common, but I've never figured out a use for them.

Blacksmith *[Chromis punctipinis]* like early mornings, when they may school, perch-like, in the shadow of your boat. They won't bite and seem to pay no attention to you, but you can sometimes catch one on a

White croaker "tom cod" [top] and queenfish "herring" [bottom].

Treefish, sometimes incorrectly called "convict bass", are found in shallow water rarely deeper than 150 feet.

tiny hook and a very small piece of squid. They are pretty, but beyond that I can't say much for them.

Garibaldi *[Hypsypops rubicundus]* the "ocean goldfish," are common to rocky areas of both the coastal and off-shore waters of Southern California. Protected by law, these beautiful orange fish may not be taken. They rarely grow larger than a foot in length but do much to enhance the underwater scene. Juvenile garibaldi are a mottled orange with brilliant blue spots. Often seen in shallow water, these fish rarely take a bait, but can occasionally be tempted with a bit of mussel or other shellfish.

Treefish *[Sebastes serriceps]*. When I worked on sportfishing boats we used to call this colorful little fish "convict bass." Incorrectly, of course, but that's how a colloquialism starts, and that is why there are Latin names for all species. Treefish are found in shallow water, rarely deeper than 150 feet. They aren't big, going to about a foot in length. They live in and around rocky areas and readily take anchovies. The basic body color is greenish-yellow to bright yellow with five or six vertical black bars and a bright red lower lip, as though wearing lipstick. Like most rock fish, treefish are excellent eating.

Needlefish *[Stronylura exilis]* is another odd fish that is sometimes taken in Southern California. They used to be common in Newport Bay and are still caught there on occasion. They are long, very slender, show an awesome set of dentures and grow to a length of about three feet. Needlefish are very difficult to see in the water as they assume the exact shade of their surroundings.

They are a lot of fun on light tackle because, if given half a chance, they will jump repeatedly when hook-ed. They are excellent eating but few people use them for food because of their appearance. They have turquoise-green teeth and bones, and the flesh has a greenish tinge until cooked.

They are quite common on long-range trips around Cape San Lucas and the offshore islands of Mexico. They hit trolled lures and live bait, and are sometimes taken in King Harbor at Redondo Beach.

Opah *[Lampris regius]* or moonfish, are uncommon but are caught from time to time along the California Coast. They are usually found with albacore and usually deep, beneath the surface-feeding fish. The last one I know of was caught in 1974 by a lady named Ida Buehler who took it while fishing for Spanish mackerel under a kelp paddy. A large opah hit one of their trolling lures as it sank under the paddy.

The opah is a spectacular fish with bright red fins, silver body with red spots, and a yellow eye. The body conformation is roughly round with a strongly forked tail. They grow to over 150 pounds but most sport catches have ranged from 40 to 60 pounds. They are strong fighters and are reputed to be excellent eating, but most specimens are mounted.

Found in warm seas, worldwide, opah have been reported from Japan, Alaska, and as far south as Cape San Lucas in Mexico. A number of these "exotics" are caught on years that albacore put in an appearance at Morro Bay.

Another ocean oddity commonly seen while fishing the waters of Southern California is the ocean sun-fish *[Mola mola]*. The sunfish or mola has no tail and only 4 fins—2 pectorals and the large dorsal and matching anal fin. The 2 large fins, by opposing action, provide their means of propulsion. These fish are really quite comical to watch as they swim because they appear so ungainly.

They are often seen lying on their sides on the surface and can easily be approached with a boat as they rarely show any fear. They do not take bait and, although they grow to great size (often over a ton), they apparently feed on plankton as they have very small mouths.

Ocean sunfish are reputed to have some food value by the Italian and Portuguese fishermen. However, when I cleaned one I could not find much that look-ed worth cooking.

These strange creatures commonly lie under or around floating kelp paddies and will take shelter in the shade of a boat when it is stopped in channel waters.

Two anglers fast to big tuna, using harness.

"What do I do with all that fish?"

Chapter 20
Long Range Fishing

Several places in this book we have discussed long-range fishing. This chapter is devoted to that type of fishing and the tackle to take. Basically, tackle used in Southern California is suitable for most long-range fishing with some additions and modifications.

The fish that will be encountered on long-range trips will range from the same species that are available to the Southern California angler to the socalled "exotics" of the tropical waters off Baja. The tropical fish include yellow fin tuna, from smaller school fish up to the record-breakers of over 300 pounds. Marlin, sailfish, black sea bass, wahoo, rainbow runners, Pacific big eyed jacks, green jacks, blue jacks, amberjacks and a multitude of grouper and other bottom dwellers can be expected.

For a number of these fish it is necessary to use wire leaders. Stranded stainless steel wire, used in conjunction with crimping sleeves, is best when trolling. For jig leaders and live bait leaders, singlestrand stainless wire, treated to darken and take away the shine, is recommended. Big fish require big bait, so an assortment of large hooks is required. A very good all-purpose hook for jigs and big bait is the Mustad Salmon hook number 9510XXX. A file or stone for sharpening hooks is a must, and since no tackle store is available, it's wise to have a good supply of "expendables" such as hooks, line, lures and wire. Big fish are all fought from a dead boat in this type of fishing, so fairly heavy tackle is required for large yellowfin tuna, marlin, sailfish, etc.

When the long-range boats get into areas of big yellowfin and billfish, light tackle has to be put in the rack and heavier rigs broken out. The minimum tackle for this type of fishing is a 4/0 high-speed Newell or Penn Senator with aluminum spool and 50-pound line. With the aluminum spool, this reel will cast 4-ounce jigs. For larger fish, I recommend a 447F Newell or 6/0 Penn Senator and 60-pound line. 60 is plenty heavy, because from a standing position it is almost impossible to break and gives added line capacity. I have found that a 9/0 is a little heavy to handle without a chair. For the giants, fish of over 100 pounds, the 50W Penn International is best, with 80 line.

A good harness is a must! I prefer the kidney style as opposed to the more common shoulder harness. I have found that in a long fight with a big tuna I can rest better in the kidney harness, and get a better lift. Wrist guards, like the ones tennis players use, help prevent bruised wrists with the larger reels. A couple pair of cheap cotton gloves help handle the fish when you get it in. A good pair of side-cutting lineman's pliers are very convenient in rigging gear and also for getting big hooks out of fish. To fish for the bottom grabbers it is sometimes necessary to get big baits down deep in heavy currents, so a supply of large sinkers is in order. A good assortment of large swivels and connectors is also handy for rigging bottom gear.

Since we rarely know exactly what fish will be encountered on any given long-range trip, it is wise to have a wide assortment of casting and yo-yo jigs along. The greatest number of jigs should be in chrome or polished aluminum. White, blue and white, and green and yellow are also good. Magic marking pens of various colors are good to change jig colors, as are small cans of spray paint.

One nice feature of long-range trips is that alcoholic beverages are carried tax free and can be purchased at "sea store prices" on the boat.

Most of these trips get either very close to, or into the tropics so sunburn can be a real problem. Take along and use some type of sunburn prevention.

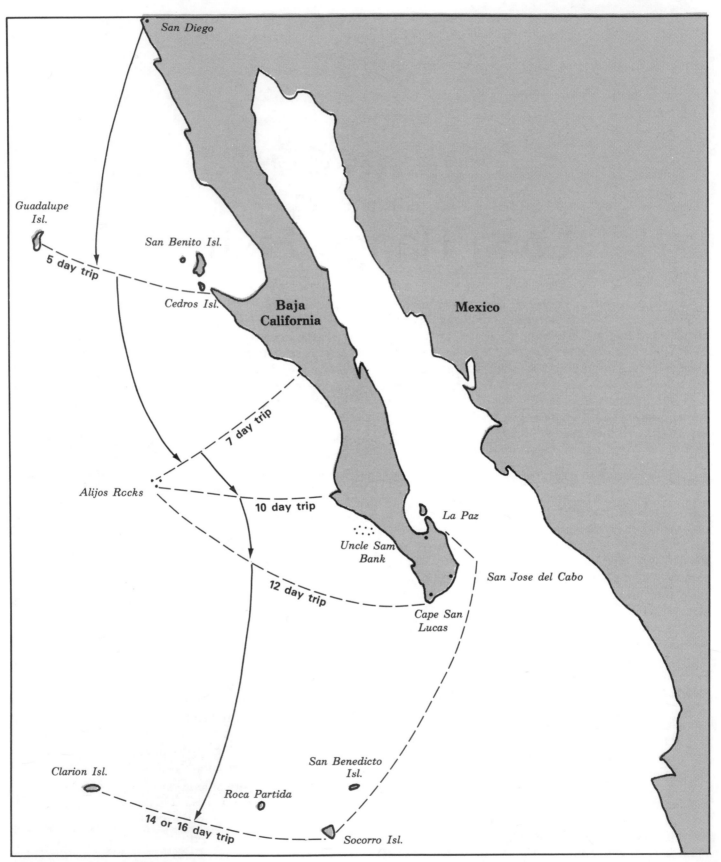

Principle long range fishing areas.

100

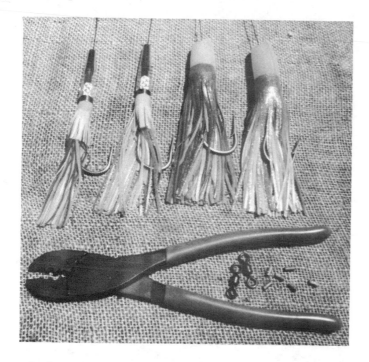

On long range trips you should take a large assortment of lures, jigs, swivels and crimping sleeves.

myself. This is not as difficult as might be supposed. All it requires is a pressure cooker and mason jars. Although I have graduated to an inexpensive canning machine and cans rather than jars. The fish is packed raw in jars or cans and cooked under 10 pounds pressure for 90 minutes to prevent botulism and produce the required partial vacuum. They keep for years. These cans, or jars, make great Christmas gifts as well as taking care of school lunches and snacks.

You may wish to have one of the "exotics" mounted. Think about this before you go on the trip and be prepared. If you ask, the crew will usually put your fish in a special part of the fish hold where it will not be damaged. Take along some old sheets and wrap it for mounting. You'll be glad you did.

I have made a number of these trips over the past several years and I have never had enough film. There are fantastic sunsets and sunrises, islands I have never seen before and fish that have to be photographed.

Those who have never made a long-range trip frequently ask "How are the fish handled?" and "What do I do with all that fish?" As each angler signs aboard he is assigned a number and a supply of waterproof cardboard tags with the number stamped thereon. These tags are stapled to the fish as they are brought aboard. Several times a day the catch is transferred from boxes on deck to the refrigerated hold for quick freezing. When the boat returns to port, frozen fish are removed from the hold and claimed by number.

What to do with several hundred pounds of prime eating fish? There are several options. Perhaps easiest, but most expensive, is to trade whole fish at dockside for canned fish. The usual rate of exchange is 1 pound of round fish for each 8-ounce can, plus so much a can. We have done this on occasion after saving out a good supply of the best eating varities for freezing and cooking fresh. The second option is to simply freeze all the catch for later use.

The third option, and the one I use most, is to freeze the catch in the local cold storage plant (most large cities have one) and at my convenience, can them

The author releasing a tagged sailfish. [Photo by Bill Beebe]

A small boy with his first fish. The fish is a good sized queenfish taken from the Seal Beach Barge.

". . .perch, bass and cabazone."

Chapter 21
Bay, Jetty, Barge and Pier Fishing

There is a lot of good fishing from and around jetties and breakwaters, as well as in the various bays of Southern California. Fishermen are permitted to walk out on many of the jetties but others must be fished from a boat. Most of them provide a good variety of fish, including perch, bass and cabezon.

These fish can be taken on either light ocean tackle or heavy fresh water gear. The rocks are rough on line and sinkers, so take lots of lead and hooks with you. For some fish, such as opaleye and black surf perch, a float with the bait suspended some three or four feet below the surface works well and saves sinkers. A long cane pole will sometimes serve as well, or better, than rod and reel for this type of fishing. Mussels are one of the best baits.

As mentioned elsewhere, kelp bass inhabit most of the breakwaters of the local area and provide some of the finest fishing for this species. Unfortunately for many people, these fish must be fished from a small boat, tight to the rocks, in the hours before dawn and after sundown.

When they are in a biting mood (and that is unpredictable), kelp bass will hit a variety of lures, including plasitc worms of various colors, skirted leadhead jigs, swimming plugs, shrimp-tail plastic lures and fresh or frozen squid, as well as plastic squid jigs. Seventeen- to 20-pound test line is recommended as these fish will be hooked right in the rocks and are quick to take advantage of cover.

Kelp bass weigh to over 10 pounds and put up a very good fight. They are among the finest eating of all West Coast fish, and best fishing often occurs after sundown on a moonlit summer evening.

Bay fishing is a calm water world where the bite is dependent on tidal flow.

Most fish available in the surf are also found in bays. In addition there are halibut, spotted sand bass, turbot, small barracuda and small white sea bass (both of the latter have size limits, and smaller fish must be released). Bay fish may be caught on the same baits as used in the surf, but spotfin croaker and turbot are particularly responsive to ghost shrimp.

In calm bay waters, light line is used along with hooks smaller than those needed in the surf. Six- and 8-pound test line is usually strong enough. Drifting among buoys and moored boats is often quite productive, as well as anchoring in one of the prime travel lanes for these fish.

Trolling for spotted sand bass and kelp bass that inhabit most of the bays is good sport and sometimes very successful. Diving freshwater plugs such as the "Bomber" are effective. Feather jigs of the single-hook type in greens, yellows, and reds are also good. Halibut will take trolled lures, but live bait, drifted on the bottom, is more productive.

For those anglers who want the thrill of big fish but wish to stay in calm water, bays provide some fine fishing for large rays and sharks. These fish are almost always taken at night, and heavy gear is required. The big bat ray *[Myliobatis californica]* reaches weights in excess of 200 pounds and is a very strong and stubborn fighter. Many anglers who pursue these fish do so simply for the thrill of the fight and then release them.

Barge Fishing

Some of my earliest and fondest fishing memories relate to barges. For as long as I can remember, except for the World War II years, there have been fishing barges anchored off the Southern California coast. At one time they were found at every fishing landing from Malibu to San Diego, as well as Catalina Island.

Most of these barges were remnants of the lumber schooner fleet that plied between the Pacific Northwest and Los Angeles Harbor. Once-proud names were reduced to the embarrassing role of anchored barges. But what a heady experience for budding young fishermen – to walk the decks of the *Minnie A. Caine,* the *Olympic,* the *Star of Scotland,* the *Billings* and many others! The *Star of Scotland* was for years a landmark off the Santa Monica pier and still carried her masts and spars. Time and storms have taken their toll of most of the old barges, but the fishing remains.

At the present time there are fishing barges operating from Redondo, Seal Beach and Belmont Pier. These are well managed, modern barges with live bait furnished and good galley service.

The are also some big sharks in the bays and one of them is very good eating. This, the leopard shark, reaches a length of about 6½ feet and a weight of over 75 pounds. For chasing this fish, you need 4/0 reels and 50-pound test line, along with a stout rod. Squid is the preferred bait, although slabs of mackerel or bonito also work well.

For the bat ray, use a very sharp hook to penetrate the bony plates of both upper and lower jaws.

The Bays

San Diego: a very large, clean harbor with lots of fish. Launching ramp.

Mission Bay: very large and extremely clean. Good small boat facilities and lots of fish. Launching ramp.

Carlsbad Lagoon: fairly small, but a top spot for croaker and other surf fish. Launching ramp.

Oceanside Harbor: small, but clean. Plenty of fish; launching ramp.

Dana Point Harbor: this produces some excellent catches from both the breakwater and small boats. Launching ramp.

Newport-Balboa: one of the finest fishing bays on the coast. Lots of large spotfin croaker, bass, halibut and other fish. Launching ramp.

Huntington Harbour: another top spot for surf fish. Launching ramp.

Alamitos Bay: lots of boats but still plenty of fish. Launching ramp.

Long Beach-San Pedro: one of the largest man-made harbors. Miles of breakwater and beaches. Good fishing. Launching ramps at both harbors.

King Harbor, Redondo Beach: Small, but with lots of fish. Bonito is the favorite here. No launching ramp, (one is in the works) but a good hoist.

Marina Del Rey: a large bay which is not heavily fished except at the mouth. Launching ramp.

Santa Monica Breakwater: the remnants of old breakwater is officially known as "the Santa Monica Reef." Good bass and perch fishing. No launching ramp.

Port Hueneme: small harbor that produces steelhead and other species in the winter months. No launching ramp or hoist.

Channel Islands Harbor, Oxnard: fairly large harbor with some good perch fishing. Launching ramp.

Redondo's barge

Ventura Harbor: at the mouth of Ventura River. Some good fishing at times. Launching ramp.

Gaviota Pier: no bay here. There is a public hoist on pier for boats up to 17 feet. This is the closest point to the northern Channel Islands and is an excellent spot for large halibut and rock fish.

Santa Barbara: small harbor with not much room to fish. However, good fishing for halibut and bass right outside harbor.

Goleta Pier: famous for calico bass, halibut and thresher sharks. Small boat hoist, 6,000-pound capacity.

Barges are usually anchored, fore and aft, over some good fishing area such as a reef or the edge of a marine canyon. The presence of the barge and the continuous supply of food gathers and holds fish. Mackerel, bonito and halibut make up the largest proportion of barge-caught fish, but some surprising catches occasionally come aboard as schools of pelagic fish pass through. The Redondo Barge, anchored on the edge of Redondo Canyon, accounts for yellowtail and even on occasion, bluefin tuna along with some good catches of bottom fish like black cod (sablefish). The barge out of Seal Beach is good for halibut and sand bass in the summer and, sometimes, good catches of barracuda along with bonito and mackerel.

Barges have many things to recommend them. Since they are large craft, motion is usually not a problem for those prone to seasickness. The barges are serviced by shore boats on a regular basis which permits the angler to come and go to suit his schedule. A barge is an excellent place to start a youngster fishing. Some barges have even introduced a night schedule during the summer months.

All barges are operated under strict U.S. Coast Guard licenses and the Bargemaster must also be licensed.

Heavy fresh water or light ocean tackle is recommended for barge fishing.

Piers

There are a great number of piers along our section of the coastline, from the Gaviota Pier on the north, to the Pacific Beach Pier almost at San Diego. These piers all provide access to some good fishing at certain times of the year. Almost all are public piers, and so exempt the angler from the necessity of obtain-

ing a fishing license, a great boon to many. At the base of most piers, right at the surf line, fish such as barred surf perch and corbina are to be caught. All along the piers, pilings provide good perch fishing for a wide variety, with piling perch the most prevalent. Sidewinder crabs are the best bait for these fish and they should be fished as close to the pilings as possible. Most of the piers have live bait available most of the year, and halibut, bonito, barracuda and occasional bass are taken in season. Night fishing from piers can provide action from sharks, rays, croakers, and sometimes lobster and crab. Pier fishing requires some special techniques. Underhand casting must be mastered as well as the method of retrieving a cast bait for halibut. Many pier anglers concentrate on smaller fish such as queenfish (herring) and smelt which may be caught on snag gangs. Mussels make good bait for most pier fishing. Many bonito fishermen have worked out a technique whereby they cast out a good sized sinker and then slide live anchovies down the line on short leaders snapped onto the main line, and thereby "flyline". It works. Refer to the chart on pages 33 and 34 for pier locations.

Piers are fine places to start young anglers, and for oldsters, too. This is the Belmont Pier, Long Beach.

Flyrod action at Redondo Beach for bonito. Exciting fishing in calm water.

106

"...both challenging and rewarding."

Chapter 22
Flyrodding

The growing sport of fishing the ocean with a flyrod is both challenging and rewarding. If you are already a flyrod fisherman in fresh water, it does not take much additional equipment to fish the salt.

Flies are simple. Large bear hair patterns and feather streamers work best. I prefer stainless steel hooks because of the rust problem encountered in salt water.

For most inshore fish, like bonito, bass and barracuda, a number 8 rod of 8½ or 9 feet is ample. A sinking line is a must, as almost all of the fish encountered prefer a fly presented well down, as opposed to one on the surface. There will be times when the fish are chasing bait on top and will take a fly on the surface, but the norm is a deep fly retrieve. Long leaders are not a necessity – 6 or 7 feet is usually enough.

Long casts are the rule in order to cover as much water as possible. For this reason many salt water flyrodders use a "shooting head" of fast sinking fly line backed with 25- or 30-pound monofilament. The shooting head is fairly short (25 or 30 feet) and has sufficient weight to pull the mono through the guides. Once mastered, the technique of casting this combination allows extremely long casts. The experts consistently cast well over 100 feet.

Another method is to use lead-core trolling line for the shooting head. I have used lead core for a number of albacore with good success. A 15-foot length of 27-pound lead core trolling line makes a fine shooting head. Braided nylon line which covers the wire core may be pushed back and the wire clipped off. This will give you a piece of line to tie on leader and backing. Lead core casts well and sinks like a stone. Both are prerequisites for albacore fishing. However, be careful of that lead core line in the wind. Keep your back cast well off to the side as it is most unpleasant to catch it in the back of the neck.

For bonito and albacore fishing a fast retrieve is usually best. Sometimes I put the rod under my left armpit and retrieve the line with both hands to get a strike. This takes a little practice and some fancy footwork when the fish is hooked. For larger fish, a size 10 or 11 rod is recommended.

The Arizona Flycasters of Phoenix have fished the upper waters of the Gulf of California for years with fly rods. They prefer a 9-foot, 10-line rod for their fishing, which is almost exclusively the surf and in the estuaries of that coast. They regularly take corvina, white sea bass, cabrilla and many other species. The fly they like best is a pattern called "Integration." This fly is tied on a long-shanked hook and consists of equal parts black and white bear hair, with the black hair covering the point of the hook and the white covering the shank. Another good fly, and one that works best for bonito, is a simple white bear hair fly on a live bait hook of the 94151 Mustad pattern with a little red nail polish on the threads. Size 2 and 4 are the most commonly used.

If you fish in Mexico, watch for dolphin and keep your fly rod handy. Many times a free swimmer will accompany a troll-hooked dolphin and they are usually a cinch to hit a fly. Leave the hooked fish in the water until the other fish hits. A wildly jumping dolphin on a fly rod is not soon forgotten.

Marlin and sailfish are now being caught on flies with regularity. The fish are teased up to the boat with hookless baits and lures and, when they are sufficiently frustrated by having the baits pulled away from them, the fly is dropped in front of them. This takes large flies, big rods and lots of line. The new, graphite fly rods work very well for ocean fly rodding because of their weight-to-strength ratio.

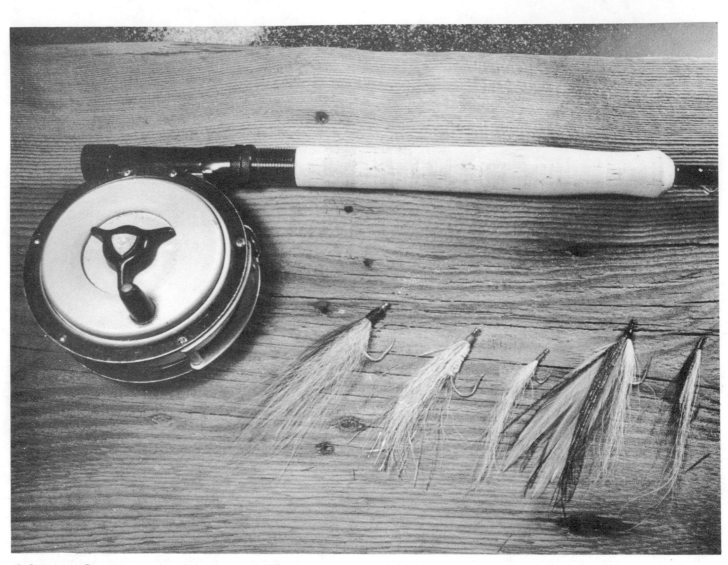

Salt water fly patterns are simple—these flies will take most species common to Southern California.

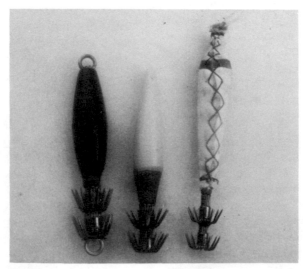

Squid catcher jigs.

Above are a number of typical salt water fly patterns. Bonito fly [upper left] and integration directly below it.

"Some of the largest yellowfin tuna ever landed were caught at night."

Chapter 23
Night Fishing

As already mentioned, some species of fish are night biters and some are not. Black sea bass are good night biters. They usually feed best in a strong to moderate current.

Barracuda will sometimes feed at night and for years there has been a good bite for these fish in the Toyon Bay area of Catalina Island from about 2 a.m. until dawn in the months of June and July. I have also made some fine catches of barracuda on the south side of Catalina in the Silver Canyon area at night. Barracuda that bite at night are usually deep and will not bite jigs—only bait.

White sea bass are a prime night fish. They are found along with squid in many cases. Kelp or calico bass sometimes hit very well in the dark. They turn on and off for some inexplicable reason. I have fished along jetties and breakwaters for bass at night without any luck and then, suddenly, had them start biting on every cast. The bite might go on for an hour, or it could continue for the rest of the night. I have found that a rising moon sometimes triggers a bite.

All sharks and rays feed at night. The bays and surf will many times produce good shark fishing, but only at night.

Albacore and bluefin tuna will sometimes come to the lights of a boat and hit very well. They don't often take a trolled lure in the dark but I have caught a few albacore by trolling "glow-in-the-dark" lures at night. They will, however, hit live bait very well at times.

A lot of surf fishing is best done at night—spotfin croaker are a prime target.

Bonito will sometimes feed at night but rarely with the abandon they display in daylight hours.

Some of the largest yellowfin tuna ever landed have been caught at night. At Soccoro and San Benedicto Islands these big tuna move in after flying fish that gather under the lights and provide some of the most exciting fishing there is. I have also caught a number of the smaller school yellowfin in the dark on jigs. Chrome seems to be the best attractor.

A double-mantle gasoline lantern is one of the best night fishing companions you can have if you do not have electricity available. This lantern gives a penetrating light that seems to draw both squid and fish very well.

Night fishing has more than its share of thrills. Large sharks will often come right to the boat, attracted by the lights. Many species of small fish, often rare, are also attracted. Flying fish, at the islands, will cruise under the lights and can easily be netted.

Phosphorescence in the water is constantly being stirred to luminescence by sea creatures, large and small. A hooked fish, first seen in this "fire" looks several times its actual size, and bottom feeders like sculpin and rays may often be seen near the surface. It's really a different world, at night.

"The fisherman's eyes in the sky."

Chapter 24
Birds

Peter Goadby in his great book on Pacific big game fishing, *Big Fish and Blue Water,* calls birds "the fisherman's eyes in the sky," and I can't say it any better.

There are many sea birds common to the fishing grounds of the West Coast and some of them are great indicators of fish. In the northern areas, large gulls like the western gull and the California gull are the most common birds and are seen wherever live bait boats are fishing. They pick up the chum and follow boats home to dine on fish scraps discarded by the crews.

A little study of bird behavior will help to locate fish. For a long time I was amazed at how quickly a large flock of gulls would congregate when feeding fish drove bait to the surface, or when a boat started to chum live bait. But it's no mystery. There are always gulls sitting on the water and a few in flight. Sometimes they are so high that it is almost impossible to see them with the naked eye, but they are there. This spread of birds provides an efficient, oceanwide information network.

When a gull in flight is just looking, it flies with a soft, easy motion, almost idling along. Watch carefully when it spots something—the wings stop moving, the bill goes down and the bird angles toward the object. If the object is alive and the gull goes after it,

there is a flash from the underside of its wings as the bird dives. This flash of wings is a signal to other birds, both aloft and at rest, that something interesting is going on. If there is more than just the initial flash of wings, birds will immediately congregate. The birds that are assembling fly with purpose, much like a shopping housewife headed for a sale. If you see either the flash of wings or birds flying with this determination, investigate.

A cloud of wheeling, diving gulls is always a sign that there is surface activity taking place. It may be game fish, sharks or mammals. A feeding seal will attract birds, but with some practice and observation you will be able to tell the difference. If the birds are all headed upwind, and are stooping to pick, it is usually a seal or garbage. But if the birds are wheeling, and more than one bird at a time is hitting the water, it's probably bait.

Watch the direction the birds are moving and try to get ahead of them with trolled lines or live bait. Don't plow through the middle of them—try to skirt the edge. If using live bait, slide in upwind and drift on them.

Pelicans, with their seemingly awkward flight and dives, are another good indicator. If the action is hot and heavy, pelicans will not climb high to dive but will

Gulls and other sea birds are great aids in locating fish.

merely get airborne and dive right back in. If the pelicans are diving from a great height, chances are that they are diving on a school of bait fish that is not right on the surface, and is not being disturbed by predators.

In late summer and fall, the most graceful of birds stop by on their annual migration to the south – the terns. These smallish birds are marked with bright red bills and coral-colored feet, and fly with a swooping flight unlike that of the gull. Terns dive into the water like junior-sized pelicans for their prey and are good fish indicators.

Offshore, shearwaters are the ones to watch. It is a pretty good bet that an area devoid of birds is also without fish. Birds may be found where there is just bait, but very rarely where there is neither bait nor fish. Shearwaters are wanderers of the open sea; winging across the swells within a feather of the surface. They are strong fliers and are constantly on the move in never-ending search for food.

Shearwaters can "fly under water" and when they find bait fish, driven to the surface by predators, they congregate, dive through the surface and swim swiftly under water to catch their food. These birds hitting the water and disappearing are a sure sign of fish offshore.

In late summer we are visited offshore by some rather exotic birds. At times, tropical birds, albatross and even frigate birds are seen in Southern California.

On down the coast, in Mexican waters, the frigate bird is one of the finest of fish indicators. This large bird is called "tijeras," or "scissors," by the Mexicans because of its long, forked tail. The frigate, also called the man-o-war bird, cannot land on water so it must pick up its fish from the surface; sometimes its does very well indeed. Frigate birds circle high over game fish waiting for surface action. Get under that circle for action of your own.

Other birds common to Mexican waters are the boobies. These birds, like shearwaters, are fast flying wanderers of the open ocean and are usually found in conjunction with schools of yellowfin tuna and skipjack. They fly over schools of fish, plummeting into the water and swimming after bait fish. When they are hitting the water, get there as fast as you can and join the fish catching.

A lone flying gull late in the afternoon, sometimes will fly over a tailing marlin, following it downswell and hope for a meal. Ralph Clock, a fine West Coast angler, and I were aboard the Tick Tock one afternoon when he found me a nice marlin this way. He saw the gull looking down and flying straight downswell. Sure enough, under the gull was a tailer. We had to run hard to get ahead of the marlin, but once ahead, a spanish mackerel in the path of the fish did the job.

In Southern California there are a number of other small sea birds that are quite common, but except for the small black petrel, they are not fish indicators. They seem to feed on minute marine organisms rather than on bait fish. The black petrel, however, is a good indication of marlin, tuna or albacore in the vicinity. An area where these birds are found should be worked thoroughly.

A closely-packed flock of shearwaters sitting and looking down into the water is another good indication of fish. Many times it is possible to raise a school of albacore by stopping on such a flock, and chumming. Fish with sinkers and don't be afraid to fish deep. Sometimes the fish are well over 100 feet down. It is also a good idea to work over a flock of sitting gulls the same way. Many times the gulls indicate recent action and if the fish have cleaned up a school of bait, they might still be around and hungry.

Properly prepared smoked fish is a delicacy.

"Some home canners add olive oil, garlic or jalapeno peppers."

Chapter 25
Now That I've Caught It

Fish furnish a great part of the world with most of its protein. Many diets currently feature fish and doctors agree that fish is one of the most healthful of foods, so—eat them.

Like the farmer, the fisherman experiences times of famine as well as time of plenty. We will not consider what should be done in times of plenty because there are innumerable cookbooks devoted to fish and seafood. We will, however, attempt to aid the angler in tiding himself over between the time of plenty.

Most fish freeze well and the dedicated fisherman would be wise to get a good freezer. I prefer the upright type as opposed to the chest because of the availability of the frozen product and the ease of defrosting.

It is possible to keep fish for long periods of time if it is handled properly at the start and packaged carefully so that no air can get to the flesh. Remember that freezing will not make a good fish out of a bad one—the quality of the fish you freeze will not be materially changed when it is thawed. So, it is important that you select only the best of fish for freezing and take good care of them, keeping them as cool as possible and cleaning them as soon as practical. *Under no circumstances should there be a delay of more than six hours before cleaning* unless they are frozen immediately. Be sure to remove all blood and viscera from the intestinal cavity, as spoilage starts there. The gills must also be removed. If possible, freeze fish with the skin on as this provides further protection. Skin them after they thaw.

According to tests made by the University of Alaska, Saran Wrap and Polyvinyl Chloride (PVC) are the best materials to use for freezer wrap. Both of these materials fit tightly and are impermeable to water and air. For fillets of smaller fish such as bass and rock cod we use half-gallon milk cartons and fill with water. This has proved to be a time saver and provides an excellent seal against air penetration. Mark contents of each carton or package and the date of freezing.

One of the best, and least understood, methods of preserving fish is canning. My Mother and Dad canned fish as far back as I can remember, and over 30 years later, I am still using their pressure cooker. In the early days they used jars. That's how I started and it is still an acceptable way of canning. I have since graduated to cans, however, for reasons I will explain later. To can fish, in either jars or cans, a bare minimum of equipment is necessary: a pressure cooker and jars or cans (if cans, you will need a canning machine), a stove and a clock.

Most smaller game fish are excellent canned. Albacore are the best, followed by yellowfin tuna, bluefin tuna, skipjack, bonito and yellowtail—in that order.

To can, fillet and skin the fish, removing any dark meat along lateral line by splitting fillet lengthwise. Put fillets into a brine of salt water (prepared with one pound of salt to five gallons of water) for about one hour. Next, cut the fish into jar or can-sized pieces and place in the container, leaving about ½-inch clearances at the top. Seal can or jar and place in pressure cooker according to manufacturer's directions, usually with one quart of water. Put the lid on the cooker with exhaust valve open and cook over

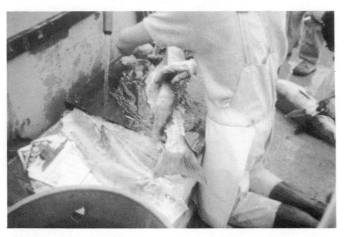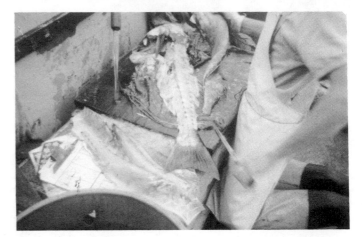

On many sport boats the crew will fillet your catch. Here a crewman demonstrates the technique for filleting a white sea bass.

Halibut are easily filleted.

Garry Black about to release a tagged yellowfin tuna. [Photo by Bill Beebe]

high heat. Allow cooker to exhaust through the pet-cock until a steady jet of steam has been emanating for seven to 10 minutes. Close exhaust petcock and bring pressure up to 10 pounds. This is equivalent to 212 degrees Fahrenheit. Regulate heat to maintain this pressure for 90 minutes and then remove from stove. (Note: It is most important to maintain this pressure for the full 90 minutes as this prevents botulism). *Important: If Using jars, allow the cooker to cool naturally—do not open the petcock—as the jars will break from the sudden temperature change!* Allow temperature indicator to return to zero and then open petcock and carefully remove lid.

If using cans, a slightly different procedure is follow-ed. As soon as the 90 minutes are up open petcock and allow all the steam to escape. Remove lid and then the cans are immediately placed in cold water to stop cooking process and complete sealing of the lids. Fish prepared in this manner is superior to most commer-cially canned fish which is precooked and all oil removed.

Home-canned fish which is packed raw in the con-tainer has all of the natural oil which provides a more moist and tender product than the commercial one. Some home canners add olive oil, garlic or

jalapeno peppers but we prefer the plain, lightly brin-ed fish.

Using cans is quicker and there is less breakage in storing and transporting of the finished product. Can-ning equipment, including cans and pressure cooker, is available in Southern California from the Container Supply Sales Company, 12571 Western Avenue, Garden Grove, California 92641, (714) 892-8321.

Smoking is yet another method of preservation although not as lasting as either canning or freezing. There are several small smokers on the market that do an admirable job. Outers Laboratories makes a fine one, as does Luhr Jensen.

Complete instructions come with these electrically-operated units and, if followed to the letter, fine eating smoked fish is assured. The longer fish is allowed to stay in the smoker, the longer it can be kept. Moisture is the enemy and the hot, dry smoke removes this moisture and flavors the fish at the same time. A hint that is not included in the instructions is to add orange food coloring to the brine for a good color—most of the commercial smokers do. A little garlic and bay leaf in the brine enhances the flavor. Marlin, all of the tuna, yellowtail and even calico bass make great smoked fish. Mackerel, when available, are also good. For the best smoked fish, bleed the fish as you catch them. It really makes a difference.

Just a word about cooking fish—but no recipes. Fish should only be cooked until the flesh loses its raw col-or, turns white (pink in the case of salmon) and flakes easily. There is no greater crime than over-cooking.

Any fish that is not going to be utilized for food, and is uninjured, should be returned to the water to fight another day and, hopefully, spawn more fish. Some fish are in trouble: marlin are pursued worldwide by longliners; all of the tunas are under terrific pressure from both the seine nets and the longliners. However, fish are a harvestable resource as well as the source of valuable protein, and no sport angler should feel

An outstanding or unusual catch makes a fine trophy to mount on the wall of office or den. This is a 158-pound yellowfin tuna.

118

any guilt about taking fish from the sea as long as it is fully utilized, and limits are observed.

Times of plenty, or when small fish are encountered, are excellent times to practice tagging. The boat crews are happy to assist and many of the boats carry large brail nets for squid which may be utilized to lift the fish from the water, thus preventing injury. The tagging program in California is now under the direction of the U.S. Department of Commerce. Tags may be obtained from the National Marine Fisheries Service, Southwest Fisheries Center, Post Office Box 271, La Jolla, California 92037.

Tagging works this way: the tag is inserted into the back, near the "shoulder" area. The polyethylene "spaghetti" portion of the tag has instructions for its return both in English and Japanese, and it also bears a serial number. There is a matching postcard which is to be mailed in after completing pertinent information concerning the fish—such as size, date of

tagging, etc. When the recapture is made, the tag is returned bearing the same information. The angler will then receive a certificate attesting to the tagging and recapture. Fishermen returning tags receive a reward of $2.00. In 1964 I participated in the program with Phil and Ralph Clock of the Fenwick Products Company on their boat, the Tick Tock, tagging a number of yellowfin tuna at Guadalupe Island. A number of the fish were subsequently recovered by American purse seiners and it was a thrill to receive the results of our efforts.

An outstanding or unusual catch makes a fine trophy to mount for the wall of office or den. I value a large yellowfin tuna taken from the waters of Soccorro and a very small roosterfish taken while surf fishing at Palmilla, Baja, California. I relive the trips each time I look at the fish.

There are two methods of fish mounting. The older way is called "skin mount" and is a process whereby

One of the best, and least understood, methods of preserving fish is canning.

the cured skin of the fish is stretched over a fiber mold and painted. The new method is to make a plaster of Paris mold of the fish and then cast a fiberglass reporduction. This method, however, necessitates getting the fish to the taxidermist whole and in good condition. If this is not possible, the fish should be carefully skinned and the skin salted for delivery to the taxidermist.

Non-Cooking Fish

We promised no recipes; but whenever we serve ceviche, sashimi or smoked fish we are asked how to do it. So, here they are:

Ceviche

Ceviche (or cebiche) is a method of cooking fish by the use of enzyme action as opposed to heat. I have run into ceviche in Mexico and Costa Rica and I understand it is on the menu in most Spanish-speaking countries of Central and South America. The principle is simple. The acid in lime juice does the cooking.

Use any white-fleshed fish such as rock fish, kelp bass, dolphin, halibut, etc. Fillet the fish and skin it. Then cut the fish into 1-inch cubes. Cover with lime juice (lemon juice may be substituted, but lime is best) and mix in the following ingredients:

To 1½ pounds of fish, add:
   1 tablespoon dry, red chili – a teaspoon salt
   2 onions, thinly sliced – 1 tablespoon cracked peppercorns
   1 clove garlic, finely chopped

Let stand for about 4 hours, or until the fish looks "cooked." Serve as an appetizer (cocktail or on crackers).

Sashimi

This is the Japanese method of eating raw fish. Don't knock it if you haven't tried it. I have eaten sashimi of wahoo, yellowfin tuna, bluefin tuna, dolphin, white sea bass and many other fish. Yellowfin and bluefin tuna are my favorites.

Fillet and skin the fish. Remove any dark meat, and chill. Once chilled, slice the fish across the grain in thin slices and arrange on a plate. Mix a sauce of Japanese soy sauce (shoyu), Coleman's dry mustard and fresh grated ginger. Mix to taste. The mustard is hot and the ginger can be overpowering if too much is used. To eat, dip the fish into sauce. Chopsticks work best.

Smoked Fish

Smoked fish makes excellent snacks and hors d'oeuvres and is easily prepared. Use only the best fish as smoking will not make bad fish good. Fillet the fish and be sure to leave the skin on as the fat is between the skin and flesh. Be sure to use collars and belly meat as they are very rich. Cut the fillets into chunks about 3 inches across. Place in a brine for 10 to 12 hours.

The brine is made as follows:
To 1 gallon of water, add the following:
   2 tablespoons fresh ground peppercorns
   ½ pound Kosher (un-iodized) salt
   4 bay leaves
   2 cloves sliced garlic
   1 large lemon, cut up, squeezed and rind added
   ½ pound brown sugar
Remove the fish; rinse in fresh water. Allow to stand until a slight glaze appears. Brush on a coat of vegetable oil and place on smoker racks. Smoke until "cooked." To preserve for a long period, smoke longer to dehydrate.

"...largest world record is a 2,664 - pound great white shark."

Chapter 26

Record Keepers

From the first days of big game fishing there has been a need to keep records of fish caught and tackle used. In the early days, many catches were not reported. Primitive boats and lack of reliable scales, combined with the relative remoteness of some fishing areas, made accurate reporting difficult, or at times impossible. The first game fishing clubs such as the Tuna Club of Avalon and the Southern California Tuna Club of Long Beach initiated the first accurate records on the West Coast. Many of these early record catches have not been surpassed to this day.

In 1939 The International Game Fish Association (IGFA) was formed and this prestigious nonprofit organization has long been recognized throughout the world. Records have been maintained for fish caught on line of 6-, 12-, 20-, 30-, 50-, 80- and 130-pound test lines for 40 species of game fish. The rules established by the association are strictly enforced, and in order for a fish to be recognized it must be weighed on scales that have been inspected within the previous six months and found to be accurate. A photograph of the fish must be submitted to the organization's headquarters together with an application listing length and girth of the fish and signed by the angler, boatman, a witness to the catch and the weighmaster. To establish the breaking strength, 30 feet of line used must be enclosed.

Record keeping performs a much-needed service to everyone interested in the resources of the sea. Declines in both quantity of the catches and size of the fish indicate a possible depletion of a specific species. The IGFA recently embarked on a program endeavoring to focus the world's attention on the health of worldwide fisheries and is doing worthwhile work in this direction. As of this writing the Atlantic bluefin tuna is the primary object of its research.

Of the species currently recognized as having world-record status, the largest fish is a 2,664 pound great white shark which was caught by Mr. Alfred Dean in Australian waters in 1959.

If you should catch a fish large enough to make "the book," have it weighed on a certified scale with witnesses present and get a good, clear photograph. Measure length of the fish from the tip of lower jaw to the fork of the tail and girth at its largest diameter. Submit this information to the IGFA. (The International Game Fish Association, 3000 East Las Olas Boulevard, Fort Lauderdale, Florida 33316). IGFA membership is open to anyone interested in sportfishing.

The records keeping for spinfishing, formerly kept by the International Spinfishing Association (ISFA), has been taken over by the International Game Fish Association (IGFA) which is accepting applications for spin caught fish.

Spinning is a challenge method of fishing and recognition for catches is made in the following line classifications: 2-, 4-, 6-, 8-, 10- and 12-pound test. Rules similar to those of the IGFA govern the records. Although I do not personally recommend spinning tackle for large offshore fish, many are caught by anglers using this technique and they esperience a great deal of satisfaction from it. Some outstanding catches listed in the current yearbook include Evelyn Fuller's 128 pound sailfish on 8-pound line and George

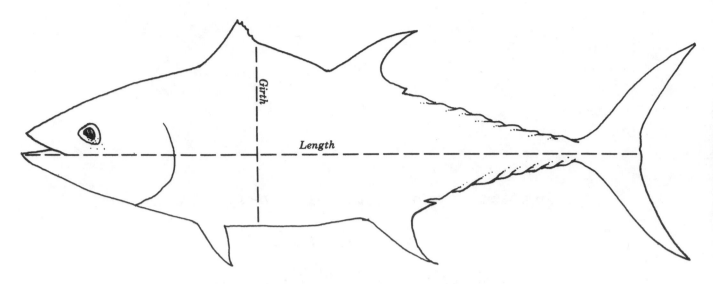

Weight by measure formula

Ramsey's 132 pound sail on 10-pound test, both taken at Mazatlan, Mexico.

Membership is ISFA or IGFA is not required for world record status.

Another organization which maintains records of salt water fish is the Salt Water Fly Rodders of America (SWFROA). Only fish caught on fly rods and by casting are recognized. Strict rules govern the tackle and its use for record purposes. Four classes of leader tippet determine records of 70 species of fish. The use of the fly rod in salt water is growing in popularity, and justifiably so. Some outstanding catches have made the fly rod a recognized tool for taking many species of big game fish. Lee Wulff's 148-pound striped marlin from Salinas, Ecuador, on 12-pound tippet and the 81-pound yellowfin tuna taken by Jim Lopez from Bermuda waters on 15-pound tippet are notable examples.

To contact SWFROA, write Salt Water Fly Rodders of America, Post Office Box 304, Cape May Court House, New Jersey 08210. Membership in this organization is open to all. A record book is published annually.

The Balboa Angling Club, another of the older Southern California fishing clubs, with membership open to all, is located next to the Balboa Pavilion in Balboa Bay. It has an official IGFA weighmaster and weigh station and keeps accurate records of the numbers and sizes of many varieties of Southern California fish.

Weight By Measure

Many times, especially for larger fish, it is convenient to know the approximate weight of a fish, without being able to weigh it. Many years ago some unknown genius worked out a formula that is pretty foolproof for most fish. The only exceptions are extremely elongated fishes such as needlefish, barracuda and wahoo. It works out very closely on all others such as tuna, marlin, black seabass etc. It works as follows:

Measure the girth of the fish at the greatest diameter and square it. Then, measure the length of the fish from the crotch of the tail to the tip of the lower jaw. Next, multiply the square of the girth times the length of the fish and divide by 800. The answer is how many pounds your fish weighs.

Example: A fish measured 38″ in girth, and 59″ in length. 38x38 = 1,444, and 59x1444 = 85,196. 85,196 ÷ 800 = 106.49 or 106½ pounds. (This formula will not work for halibut-like fishes, either.)

Since the first printing of this book, the IGFA has taken over all of the records keeping for both spinfishing and salt water fly rods records.

The Fish

Since this book is dedicated to the Southern California fisherman, I have endeavored to include all of the prominent fish, as well as some of those not so prominent. For identification of those not-so-common species, I recommend *Fish Bulletin Number 157, Guide To The Coastal Marine Fishes Of California.* This paperback book is available from: Publications, Division of Agricultural Sciences, University of California, 1422 South 10th Street, Richmond, CA 94804.

This book contains excellent black and white illustrations of just about all the fish that may be encountered along the California coastline. My listing is only of those fish that are regularly taken by hook and line sportsmen.

SOUTHERN CALIFORNIA ANGLERS' LEXICON: A TO Z

1. THE FISHING TOOLS:

   A. *Backlash:*
   The snarl of line which occurs with conventional reels when improper casting techniques are used. (slang: "overrun")

   B. *Bait:*
   Anything (other than artificial lures) which is used on the hook to make the fish bite. May be live or dead and parts thereof.

   C. *Belt Socket:*
   A leather belt with cup to hold butt of rod in position at the waist and to prevent injury.

   D. *Butt:*
   The bottommost part of the rod.

   E. *Conventional Guide:*
   Small diameter guide for use with revolving spool reel.

   F. *Conventional Reel:*
   Reel with revolving spool. Most favored for all but the smallest fish.

   G. *Drag:*
   A feature of a reel that acts as an adjustable brake; allowing varying tensions so that a fish may run without putting the reel in free spool.

   H. *Free Spool:*
   A feature of a reel, allowing the spool to turn freely without the handle turning.

   I. *Gaff:*
   A hook(s), usually fastened to a pole, to lift fish (which are too large to be lifted on the tackle used) from the water. May be a weighted set of hooks on a rope (pier gaff) or a detachable hook on a pole with rope (flying gaff).

   J. *Gangion:*
   A leader with a number of hooks on short leaders – usually for bottomfish.

   K. *Guide:*
   That which is fastened to the rod at intervals to "guide" the line along the length of the rod. May be of various sizes and conformations.

   L. *Jigs:*
   Lures for casting or trolling. Feather jigs, psychedelic jigs, bone jigs and the so-called "candy-bar" type "iron".

   M. *Leader:*
   Any material used between the end of the line and the lure or hook. Usually wire of heavy monofilament.

   N. *Line:*
   The connection between the angler and the fish; that which is on the reel. Line may be of many different materials such as monofilament (the most common), dacron, braided or twisted nylon, silk, or even wire. (Slang: "string").

   O. *Lucky Joe:*
   A light gangion with small, sharp hooks with yarn or feathers. Used to catch bait such as mackerel or squid.

P. *Needle Nose:*
Long-nosed pliers, usually with a side cutter, used to remove hooks from fish and to cut monofilament and wire. Should be carried in a leather sheath.

Q. *Pole:*
The same as the rod except that no reel is attached, nor are there any guides. As in cane pole, lift pole, etc.

R. *Reel:*
That which holds the line.

S. *Rod:*
Upon which the reel is attached to provide an extension for casting and also for playing the fish; acts as a shock absorber. (Slang: "stick").

T. *Roller Guide:*
Guide with revolving roller(s) used to decrease friction and wear on line – usually in big game fishing. (Not for casting).

U. *Sinker:*
A weight, usually of lead, used to take the bait or lure to a desired depth. May be chromed or painted for attraction. (Slang: "lead").

V. *Spinning Guide:*
Large diameter guide to accommodate the revolutions of the line as it comes off the spinning reel. (May be used with conventional reels)

W. *Spinning Reel:*
A reel with a fixed spool (one which does not revolve), which allows the line to "spin" directly off the spool without the friction of a revolving spool. (Allows casting of very light baits or lures without the possiblity of backlash).

X. *Star Drag:*
The adjustment piece on the reel to control the amount of drag.

Y. *Tip:*
The top end of the rod.

Z. *Tip Top:*
The end guide at the tip of the rod.

2. FISHING TERMS:

A. *Auxiliary:*
Secondary engine(s) to provide electrical power on a boat.

B. *Breakwater:*
Man-made bulwark against the sea. It is usually rock and may or may not be connected to land.

C. *Cast:*
The act of using the rod and reel to throw the bait or lure a distance from yourself. It may be overhead, sidearm or underhand.

D. *Cattle Boat:*
Uncomplimentary slang denoting an open-party sportfishing boat.

E. *Chart:*
Sea map.

F. *Charter Boat:*
Passenger carrying sportfishing boat not engaged in the daily trade must be "chartered." Is usually a limited load boat.

G. *Chum:*
That which is put into the water to attract and stimulate fish to feed. May be live bait, dead fish or mollusks, or parts thereof. (Chumming)

H. *Chumline:*
The string of chum which falls behind the boat from either the boat's movement or the action of the wind or the current.

I. *Deck:*
The floor of a boat.

J. *Drift:*
To fish without the use of the anchor. Usually, "we made a drift."

K. *Galley:*
The kitchen on a boat.

L. *Harbor:*
Calm, protected area. Usually behind a breakwater or jetty.

M. *Head:*
The bathroom on a boat.

N. *Jackpot:*
Money put into a pool for the largest fish. (Check local rules such as, "no Sharks," "no Halibut," "no trolling fish," etc.)

O. *Jetty:*
Man-made rock breakwater protruding into the sea. Usually at a right angle to the shore.

P. *Knot:*
A unit of sea speed – "the boat averaged ten knots." A sea mile, or "nautical Mile", is equal to 6076 feet, or 1-1/8 miles.

Q. *Landing:*
Sportfishing operation. May be from a pier or dock.

R. *Main Engines:*
A boat's propulsion engines.

S. *Meter:*
A sonar device for measuring the depth of water beneath the hull of a boat. Also an echolocator of fish – may be flasher, graph readout or digital.

T. *Pump:*
The act of raising a fish by alternately raising the rod and then reeling down as far as possible. (Short pumping is the method used by most experienced fishermen, applying the maximum pressure to the fish by a rapid, rhythmic, pumping action. Also called "short stroke"). (Slang for pump: "stroke")

U. *Skunked:*
No fish.

V. *Strike:*
A fish biting the lure of bait.

W. *Throwing Iron:*
Slang for casting a jig, as opposed to yo-yo.

X. *To Strike:*
The act of attempting to set the hook in the fish by pulling back on the rod, sharply.

Y. *Troll:*
To drag lures or baits behind a moving boat. NOT TRAWL.

Z. *Yo-Yo:*
A drop a jig, or lure, to the bottom or thereabouts and either retrieve or jerk up and down like a yo-yo.

3. THE BAITS (and the Fish): (All baits called by local name)

A. *Anchovy:*
(Engraulis Mordax) The common bait used in the live bait fishery. Almost all species will take Anchovies.

A.1. *Salted Anchovies:*
A poor substitute for the fresh or frozen bait but, sometimes effective for Halibut and other bottom feeders.

A.2. *Meatball:*
A dense school of baitfish usually anchovies, driven to the surface and being preyed upon by predators such as tuna or albacore, many times accompanied by large flocks of birds, sometimes called "bird schools".

B. *Barracuda:*
One of the best baits for Black Sea Bass and Broadbill.

C. *Blood Worms:*
The worms, available at the local bait stores, come from the East Coast – flown in. They make very good bait for most surf fish.

D. *Bonito:*
Same uses as for Barracuda. Also good slab bait.

E. *Clams:*
All are good baits for surf fish.

F. *Common Shrimp:*
Good bait for most small rock rish.

G. *Flying Fish:*
(Cypselurus Californicus) A Marlin bait – usually trolled.

H. *Ghost Shrimp:*
A local Mud Shrimp that is sold alive by the bait shops along the coast. Best bait for Croaker and Corbina in the bays.

I. *Giant Squid:*
Imported large Squid, up to three feet in length, are used for Broadbill.

J. *Green Mackerel:*
(Scomber Japonicus) A good bait for Yellowtail, White Sea Bass, Black Sea Bass, Marlin and Broadbill.

K. *Green Moss:*
At certain times of the year, green moss is the best bait for Opaleye. This moss may be gathered in back bays and sloughs at low tide.

L. *Grunion:*
(Leuresthes Tenuis) Excellent bait for Yellowtail and Calico Bass.

M. *Herring:*
(Seriphus Politus) Not a Herring, but the same family as Tom Cod. Is also excellent bait for Calico Bass and Halibut.

N. *Mussels:*
Bi-valve Mollusks found on rocks, pilings and docks at, or below, the midtide line. Very good bait for all varieties of surf and rock fish.

O. *Octopus:*
When bottom fishing, many times a freshly caught fish will disgorge a small Octopus. Always use this for bait.

P. *Peas:*
Frozen green peas are sometimes an effective bait for Opaleye.

Q. *Perch:*
At times small Perch will be found in the bait tank with the Anchovies. They may be the "Walleye" or the "111" or the "Lemon Perch" – all are good bait for Calico Bass.

R. *Razor Clams:*
Locally caught small Clam. Good bait for surf fish.

S. *Red Rock Shrimp:*
A local bait – sometimes hard to come by. When available, a best bait for all Rock Perch, Opaleye, and Blue Perch.

T. *Sand Crabs:*
The locally caught Sand Crabs are sometimes the best bait for surf fish, particularly the large Surf Perch. Softshell Sand Crabs, when available, are better than hardshells.

U. *Slab Bait:*
A fillet of fish with the skin on. Used whole for a variety of fish – a good bait for Rock Cod, large Yellowtail and Black Sea Bass.

V. *Smelt:*
In the smaller sizes, an excellent bait for Yellowtail and Calico Bass.

W. *Spanish Mackerel:*
(Trachurus Symmetricus) Not a real mackerel – a member of the Jack Family. Good bait, at times, for Yellowtail, Calico Bass and Marlin.

X. *Squid:*
(Cephalopoda) The most universal bait. All fish eat squid except for the very few vegetarians. It is the preferred bait for Yellowtail, White Sea Bass, Calico Bass and bottomfish.

Y. *Sugar Cured Mackerel* (Bonito):
A best bait for surf Perch.

Z. *Tom Cod:*
(Genyonemus Lineatus) Not a Cod, but a member of the same family as the White Sea Bass. It is usually considered a trash fish but, in the smaller sizes, makes an excellent bait for large Calico Bass.

[Photo by Bill Beebe]

132

About The Author

J. Charles (Charlie) Davis, III, was born in Southern California in 1928 and started fishing "before he can remember." At the age of five he caught tuna and yellowtail from the San Diego sportfishing boats – and has been fishing ever since. He began working on the boats while in high school and, at eighteen (the earliest permissible age), obtained his Coast Guard operator's license and started running charter boats to Catalina Island.

He continued, alternating with commercial fishing in the off-season, until 1957 when he quit the ocean for a career in the fishing tackle industry as a wholesale salesman. Later he became a manufacturers' representative for a number of the leading tackle companies – the position he holds today. As a representative he continues his fishing and also assists in research and development of new products and techniques.

Charlie has owned his own commercial fishing boat and fished swordfish commercially. His present boat is a 38-foot Luhrs Sportfisher, which he uses in Southern California and Mexican waters.

He has done it all! He has fished the waters of Southern California and nearby Mexico for fifty years, the west coast of the Californias from Point Conception to Cape San Lucas, and on into the gulf. He has also made six trips to the Revillagigedo Islands and on three of those trips caught what proved to be the largest yellowfin tuna registered in the annual Field & Stream contest, on 50-pound test line. He was the first angler to hold a world record for yellowtail on 3-thread linen line. Currently, he holds the world record for flyrod-caught albacore.

Charlie Davis is an enthusiastic angler who enjoys sharing the knowledge he has gained during his long career. He inaugurated a salt water fishing class a Long Beach City College where he taught a 16-week accredited class, for three years, and now teaches at Golden West College, in Huntington Beach.

Charlie's parents, Mary and J. Charles Davis, II were pioneers in local salt water fishing circles and were on radio for many years with weekly fishing reports. In the late forties, they presented the nation's first television program devoted to fishing. Charlie and his wife Helen have three children – Diann, Steve and Mark. Fishing has truly been and continues to be the life of this family.